UNIVERSITY ACRES
AND
HIGHLAND SCHOOL

*****

A HISTORY

Julia Hawkins and Constance Navratil

Baton Rouge, 2004

Reprinted, 2012

ISBN 0-615-12778-9
January, 2005

Baton Rouge

Claitor's Publishing Division

UNIVERSITY ACRES - A HISTORY

I

University Acres exudes a certain charm that is hard to define. To begin with, its convoluted borders center around a circle that interrupts the flow of Sunset Boulevard towards its end and sets up a unique street plan that characterizes the neighborhood. It is a joy to joggers and a plague to the uninitiated deliveryman. The subdivision straddles Highland Road and runs from Bayou Fountain deep into Bayou Duplantier. Sunset Boulevard with its broad reaches and attractive plantings is an invitation to explore; another entry from Highland Road, Nelson Drive, is invitingly canopied with a noble stretch of live oaks, and Leeward Drive once edged the nursery owned by the Polizottos which provided much of the trees and shrubbery that bejewel the subdivision. There is no doubt that "the Acres," as it is affectionately known, abounds in great trees, an abundance of flowering shrubs and homes that display great architectural variety, a special quality that adds to its uniqueness and charm. And what other subdivisions in Baton Rouge can boast of a school, a church and a park! But what else is there that has forged a sentiment in its residents that reaches into the past?

The first filing was made in 1923 by Berlin E. Perkins' 'The Pelican Realty Co.' from land originally owned by the Sam McConnell family. The McConnell plantation of 300 acres of cotton and corn, originally a Spanish land grant in the eighteenth century, was called "China Grove" after the chinaberry trees that grew there. Mr. Perkins gave the streets flowery names even though the land was quite fallow. Claude

Grenier who was a physics professor at LSU and hailed from France and Helen, a school teacher who at some point taught at Highland, discovered in a shed on their property at 715 Leeward Drive, where Prewitt Nelson used to live, one of these road signs, "Sycamore" which they showed to Acres historian, Julia Hawkins. Nelson Drive was Sycamore Drive, Sunset was Main Drive, Leeward was Oak Drive, Menlo was Myrtle Drive, Boone was Nelson Drive and Guava was Pecan Drive.

Highland Road was a gravel road to LSU and dirt roads culled from the McConnell plantation defined the subdivision. Bill Stracener remembers seeing the bumpy rows of furrows in his side yard. Behind the home of Jackie Cole at 5894 Guava is an old smoke house left over from the McConnell plantation and when they first moved in, there was still a barn and an ancient refrigerator car from the time of Harry Boone Nelson's days. University Acres was incorporated into the City of Baton Rouge by the time of the second filing by Nelson Brothers Contractors. Street names were changed, some to eliminate duplications in the city and family names won out – Nelson, Chandler (a brother), Boone, and the bookkeeper, Dubois. Mrs. J. P. Nelson returned from a trip to California and contributed California names – Sunset Blvd. and Menlo.

The Claitor family, of the publishing and law book firm, now lives in the McConnell's China Grove home at 5925 Highland Road. In 1962, Gertrude McConnell Preston was contacted for information on the McConnell home where she had lived as a child. The home was owned by her grandmother, who inherited it from her father, John B. Kleinpeter. It consisted of three rooms across and two rooms deep. There were wide porches the entire length of the front and back of the house. Union

Grenier Residence-715 Leeward:
The old Prewitt Nelson home.

Old street names found in —

The Real Estate Shed at 715 Leeward.

Claitor Residence-5925 Highland Road – The original China Grove Plantation McConnell home.

Old smoke house of the McConnell Plantation behind the Cole Residence-5894 Guava Dr.

General Benjamin Butler used it during the Civil War siege of New Orleans. The kitchen and storeroom stood about ten feet directly back of the house, connected to the main house by a covered porch. There was a staircase going up from the center back room into an attic with two rooms: the largest, in which she and her sister used to play, was used for storage; the smaller room served as an extra bedroom when needed. These memories pre-date 1906, when Gertrude's family moved into Baton Rouge and her father, having been trained as a sugar chemist at L.S.U., would go to Cuba for the sugar seasons. Such are the beginnings of our history.

II

The impetus for the expansion of South Baton Rouge came with news, in 1925, of the impending move of Louisiana State University to its present location. Highland Road, once the high ground trail of Indians that threaded through woods and farmland (the large magnolia at 239 Nelson Drive was transplanted there as a sapling from Bayou Duplantier and yielded an Indian arrowhead under its roots when moved), became a stomping ground for developers and there sprang up subdivisions to meet the needs of a university neighborhood. Growth was slow at first with perhaps ten or twelve homes and a scattering on Highland Road. Mr. W. L. Childress acted as agent for Mr. Perkins and sold a lot for $600 to a then student Joe Richard who finally built a house in 1929 on Sunset Blvd., the rest of that block being owned by Mr. James Thomas. Joe and Jackie Richard turned out to be great gardeners. Joe taught in the LSU Agriculture Department and as an authority on the iris was President of the Iris Society. He named a hybrid iris "Midshipman" for his son Jack who was at Annapolis.

On April 18th, 1938 Harry Nelson held an auction at University Acres to sell lots, setting aside portions for a potential school site. Blueprint maps were distributed for prospective buyers and it was advertised as "Country Living" with music, balloons and an auctioneer. A large tent was erected, similar to the traditional practice the Nelson family remembered from their boyhood days around Lexington, Kentucky. Some lots brought $200, others were withdrawn when bids were too low, but enough were sold to get things going again ahead of the coming war. In 1940 few houses, including those on Highland Road, were listed from the Acres in the City Directory that year. Now there are more than 240 homes in the Acres. Residents who go back to those early days recount the farm-like existence.

Bill Stracener recalls Mr. And Mrs. Childress on Highland Road and their three children, Michael, Ruth and Robert. They had registered milk cows and sold milk and eggs. She had weekly prayer meetings at her house, attended by many in the neighborhood and was a much-loved teacher both at the old Highland and the current Highland school. Mr. Jefferson, who helped develop lots on the Bayou Fountain side of Highland Road bulldozed the headstones of an old cemetery down into the bayou near Robert and Josie Taylor's property at 6040. He had a small dairy east of the circle on Chandler and Bob Childress herded his cattle for him. A faculty member of the dairy department also kept a cow at 655 Nelson Drive and Bill's father had horses, cows, a calf, a pig and prize Rhode Island Red chickens. The Stracener house built in 1926, - it was later moved to 337 Nelson Drive and became the home of the Annis family, Yvonne and her late husband Grey, such good neighbors - was shielded from the animals by a thick cane break, dug up after WW II when the Straceners built a new

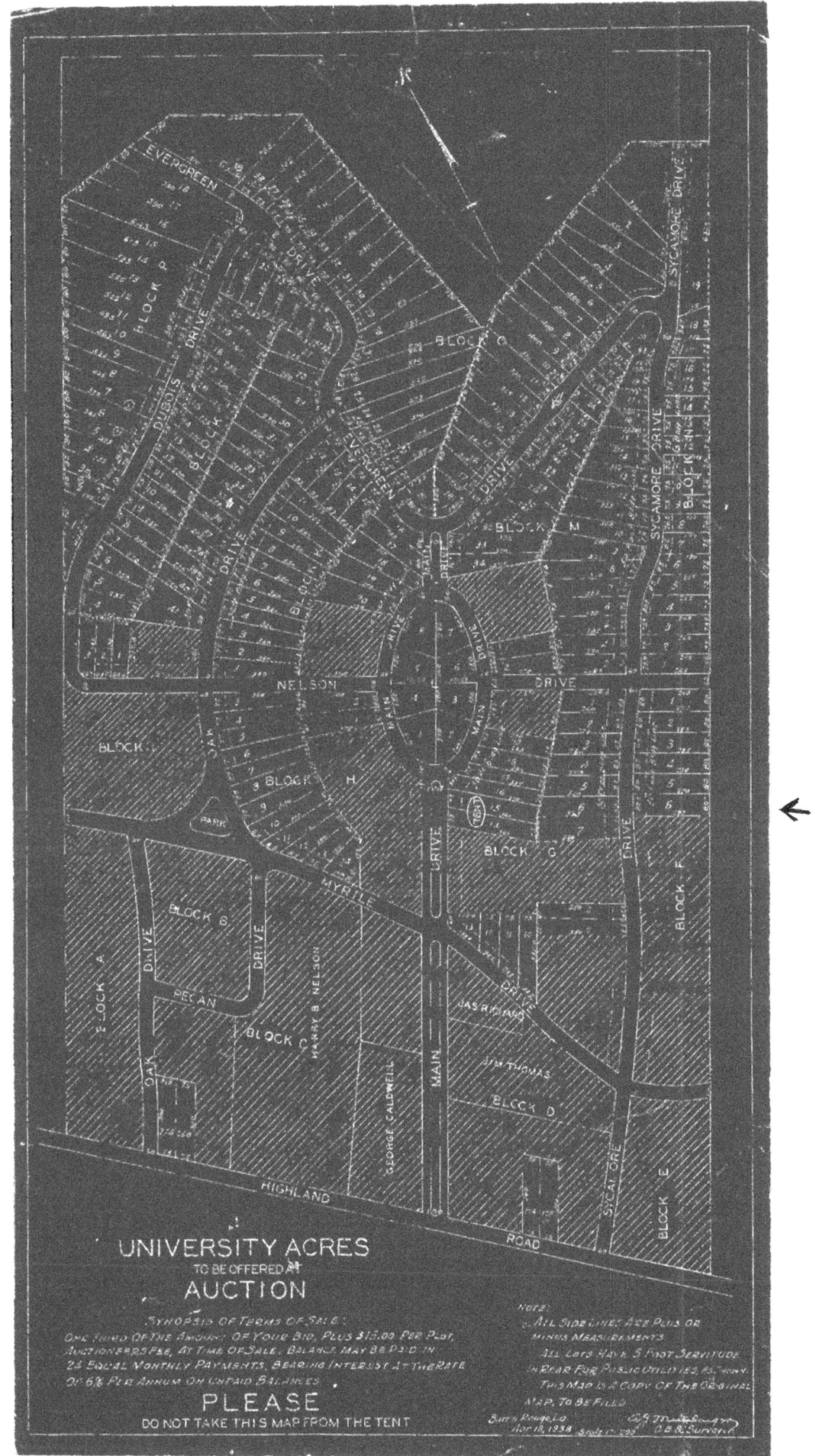

Map of University Acres distributed at 1938 auction, showing location of the Nelson Bros. Tent.

W.L. Childress Residence-Lots 5 & 6 Highland Road

5884 Chandler Dr.: The Greek Revival home of Dr. C. Creed on land acquired from Dr. M.B. Sturgis who planted the oaks.

210 Sunset Blvd. – THEN   The residence of Joe Richard.

210 Sunset Blvd. – NOW.   The residence of Frank Holthaus.

house, but at that time it became a roost for hundreds of raucous redwing blackbirds that made a deafening sound morning and evening! Bill also recalls that when Mr. Thomas built the Dutch barn at the corner of Nelson and Menlo, his father planted a row of sasanquas and camellias to assuage the smells of stable cleanings dumped out along Menlo! And farming could be hazardous. The annual burn off of the Fisher place (now Woodstone) came dangerously close to his uncle's house on Nelson and would be staved off with a bucket brigade to stop the flames. It was during these depression years that his father's gate posts had markings for the transients – meaning 'you can get something to eat here' and 'no sleep here'. The hospitableness of "country folk" would be the legacy of the Acres folk. Ruth Murray, born the year the Acres was opened, lived across from the Claitor home on Highland and recalls that her mother taught at Highland School and that they kept cows, chickens and had fruit trees in the garden. Robert and Velma Johnson moved into 5834 Boone in 1959 and they had a veritable farmyard. The grown family, a landscape architect, a doctor, a paralegal, a real estate appraiser (who provided the Acres with a great map) all remember the miniature red barn and they had pigs, a horse, a baby bull that they bought at an auction and kept until it weighed 700 lbs., chickens and guinea hens, rabbits, and a pet goat that had the run of the house. (Mr. Johnson said they always wanted to get a zebra, an unfulfilled wish!) Ruth Hyatt also recalls that several residents who worked at Ethyl Corp. and carpooled, leaving the Acres at 7 a.m., were picking up "the guys" when a pig ran across the street in front of the car. "It turned out to be one of the numerous pets the Hawkins had". Mr. Nelson once imported a buffalo to try cross-breeding on his land near Ben Hur road. Mildred Dubois kept a horse, as did the Cretinis at 732 Leeward. Dr. Edward Lambremont, who was the Director of the Nuclear Science Center at LSU, his wife Jane and family kept a Shetland pony that occasionally would roam the neighborhood, as Winston and Bernadette Day were to find out soon after they moved in on Menlo. And the Navratils built a substantial barn behind their house, courtesy of the landowner, Robert Easterly, for their daughter's horse. This was in the "forest primeval" behind Nelson Drive where tree houses abounded until suburbia caught up with it. It was into "The Woods" behind Chandler, Dubois and Nelson that Betty Bollinger remembers going on nature hunts led by Dougie Hitt who was Bluebird and Camp Fire Girl leader for years; they met every Wednesday afternoon at her home and would work on various awards.

One of the earlier settlers at 5929 Menlo, Wick Babin (whose wife Ruby was a 1st Grade teacher at Highland), was in charge of the rodeos at L.S.U. which was an exciting event for all concerned. Later on, the Circle N Ranch, on land which had been owned by Harry Nelson in the 30's, would hold fond memories for Hazel Hardy Swyers, who ran the ranch and lived at 508 Sunset Blvd. and remembers the horse show events and competitions and sleep-overs and endless rural roads and trails to explore. Prior to his death, Mr. Nelson entertained guests at a round- roofed structure which had a merry-go-round for entertaining the children. Cora and Brooks were his employees living on the property and remained after Mr. Nelson's death and were loved by all. The ranch had a goat mascot, Charlie Brown, which was dressed in a Circle N blanket and hat with a white plume for parades. One rodeo parade when he tired, he rode with the Queen in the back seat of a convertible; he was also famous for eating up the oil field log book records one night.

Yes, oil was struck! In the mid to late 30's, drilling started with its constant clamor and gas flares that lit the night sky and brought hope of some pay-off. Vira Mae Kelton Harvey remembers a night they started drilling for oil. It was an excitement for the children, many of whom went to Highland School and one was in Mrs. Gamble's Nursery in the Acres. In the late 30's when oil exploration began, Marie Standifer states that the explosions would shake the whole neighborhood. The first well was drilled on Guava Drive (property that would later belong to Al Moreau); later, another major company drilled a well on the corner of Leeward and Boone. As Bill Stracener tells it: "The company engaged an Acres resident lawyer to get the leases signed, but he formed a new corporation and split up the leases, hoping the major company would buy out everything – making a killing for himself! The major company abandoned the project and the lawyer soon moved away. Records at the Department of Natural Resources show that the oil pool extended under Menlo to Nelson and was eventually drained by the well on Leeward and Boone."

The oldest house on Sunset was built in 1924/25 by the Murrays on the corner of Menlo. The gate posts and fountain basin are all that remain. The Becker house, now the home of Joe and Merle Suhayda, was moved to 285 Sunset from Highland Road in the 1930's to make room for the Jackson house, 5800 Highland, involved in the scandals of the use of LSU materials. Mrs. Becker, a friend of Huey P Long, was the organist at Sacred Heart Catholic Church and taught piano at Highland School. Mr. Becker was Director of the State Retirement System. Ory Poret married their daughter Sarah and they built just behind at 5976 Menlo. As a WWII veteran, Ory is very active in the American Legion and was always interested in the Acres activities. The Pugh residence at No.167 was built in 1929 for a professor of Agronomy, Mr. Kreager who planted many of the native Louisiana plants around his house, and the ginko tree which has brought such pleasure to distinguished law professor George Pugh and his wife Jean – the suggestion to settle on Sunset Blvd. came from friends of theirs, Prof. Veltrop who lived at 6025 Chandler   The first house on the other side of Sunset was built by Joe Richard, followed by the unique home of Mr. Thomas at No.158 who owned much of that property.   His house was prefabricated, made of ¼" steel that was shipped by barge from St. Louis on the Mississippi.   Mr. Thomas was a friend and construction consultant for Huey P. Long and who's to say – in view of the violent end of the governor – that the Kingfish had not expressed an interest in a bullet-proof house, and this was proof that there was such a thing!   It came with a steel swimming pool and Babs Thomas would have sorority parties there.   A former owner remembers that to make a door from a window a blow torch was used and when roofers were adding a peaked roof to the original flat roof, the contractor remarked that it was a "fortress". And a lightning rod was a requirement.   The front door had a small "stoop", there was a chain-link fence and many azaleas.   That was in the early 30's and Hays Town made subsequent changes to the exterior, which is now the home of Dr. Steve and Margaret Brookshire.   (There is a house on Dubois that has a bomb shelter beneath it – residue of the "Cold War" of the 60's.)   C. L. Stracener built the two-story Haymaker house at 254 Nelson in 1926 (the apartments at the back were added later) and Prof. Stanley Preston, who was an expert ham radio operator, built his home at 672 Nelson Drive in 1936.   He and Thes had his father live with them who is fondly remembered for making baskets out of pine needles that he made for charity.   His

The oldest house on Sunset Blvd., built by the Murrays at the corner of Menlo – the gate posts and fountain basin are all that remain.

Suhayda Residence-285 Sunset Blvd.: The Becker house moved from Highland Road

Pugh Residence-167 Sunset Blvd.: - the Kreager house.

Brookshire Residence-158 Sunset Blvd.: - the Thomas house.

The bridge connecting neighbors on Nelson Dr. under snow, Feb.'73.

colleague, Mr. O'Day in the Forestry Department, built 658 Nelson Drive in 1937. The two houses are separated by a swale, and a wooden bridge was built over the ravine to make visiting easier. A later owner of the O'Day house was Dr. Grover Murray who, apart from being an internationally recognized geologist, cultivated camellia varietals as a hobby. On being appointed to the Presidency of Texas Tech in Lubbock he took some of his potted camellias from the Acres for him and his wife Nancy to enjoy. The ravine, at the back end of Dubois, as Marie Standifer reports it, has been treated by various occupants in different ways; some ignoring it, some modifying it, and others turning it into a beautiful natural landscape. In the 1960's a young lawyer who had grown up there returned to visit and remembers his friends had dammed up the ravine and had had a fish pond there. One day in the late 40's the boys noticed that a thin film of oil was forming on their pond and soon all the fish were dead. Not long after, a swimming pool was built in the back section of Leonard and Chookie Platt's home at 735 Dubois and all the construction was done by hand – the hole dug out, dirt and even cement brought in by wheelbarrows!

With the end of the war, veterans were returning to civilian life and there were still shortages of materials and labor for house building. Some bought lots and bit by bit, built their own homes and helped each other. Julia Hawkins still marvels that her ex-Naval Lieutenant physicist husband could build their house with little or no constructional help except her own! But wartime living makes for enterprising turns of fate – Lieut. Murray Hawkins was at Pearl Harbor at the time of the attack and could not get back for a marriage ceremony so he and Julia were married by telephone, which is quite a war story. It was a Jewish Rabbi who officiated with Murray in Hawaii, whilst a Baptist minister and Julia were on the only two telephone lines in a Ponchatoula building – the Guaranty Trust Co. – and by this means the Episcopalian couple were pronounced man and wife. Murray and Julia have lived in the Acres since 1949. Murray Hawkins was head of the Petroleum Engineering Department at LSU.

Just after the war, Leslie and Garnet Glasgow and their three sons settled in on Sunset. She was one of the most beloved of Highland School teachers and Leslie, on the faculty of Wild Life Management at LSU who later headed Wildlife and Fisheries, was Asst. Secretary in the U.S. Department of the Interior in Washington and was in charge of all national parks and monuments. He was "outstanding Naturalist of the Year and brought distinction to LSU" - and to the Acres. Nick and Elnora Carter felt the Acres were pretty wild and woodsy when they bought their lot on Dubois. They used to drive out to picnic on it and do a little clearing in preparation for building.

Houses have also been moved into the Acres. Louisiana Supreme Court Judge Fred and Polly Blanche moved the residence on 6222 Highland Road from its original site on the lake near LSU. The owners were pleased to give it, to be rid of it and Polly was truly gifted in architectural and interior design. They paid $3,500 to have it moved in 1958 onto the lot on Highland they had bought for $15,000. (It was later sold to Roger Richardson). Polly's son Robert loved his 2nd Grade teacher, Jean Simmons, and for Christmas had his mother buy a special 'angel' present. Later when his cousin married Jean, Robert would always say that he had been the first to fall in love with her. Will and Melanie Jones moved his father's house to its new location on 843 Dubois Drive. Don Fuson brought the beautiful 1803 plantation home, which once stood where the Sunshine Bridge in St. James Parish now stands, to 5957 Menlo Drive.

Moved to 6222 Highland Road – the residence of Judge Fred Blanche.

Moved to 843 Dubois Dr.: - the Jones' relocated their family house.

Union Plantation, built 1803.

Moved to 5957 Menlo –
The residence of Don Fuson

Built in 1803 on the bank of the Mississippi facing the river, it was originally two stories with a solid brick base and cypress second floor. Marcus Bringier owned much of the land thereabouts in the late eighteenth century and presented it to his daughter Elizabeth in celebration of her union with Augustin Tureaud, hence its name, Union Plantation. Their son, in building Tezcuco Plantation, stipulated that the mouldings and fireplaces be identical to his parents' home. From those plans fortunately archived, Don Fuson was able to restore Union Plantation with his master carpenter Cecil Patin to its former state, for the home had undergone many movings before he bought it from Mrs. Potts in 1992. In 1926, the brick ground floor had been demolished, moved by mule and logs, and rebuilt as a single-story raised cottage, to make way for the building of the levee. Its four dormer windows in the attic bedroom area caught the breezes from the river. It was moved again as Texaco bought the property, and has found its final resting place in the Acres. It has the original windows, pegged doors and the tongue-and-groove cypress siding is very rare. (There is also a Persac drawing of Union Plantation on which the landscaping is based). Dr. Bill Hines and his wife Bunny Prosser Hines also chose the Acres, in which Bill had grown up, for the relocation of a cypress house believed to have been built around 1894 at St. Hypolite Street (535 North Sixth Street), downtown Baton Rouge. With the assurance of carpenter Thomas Darensbourg that the materials were in excellent shape, the two-story 4,800 sq. ft. dwelling with 12 ft. ceilings and sweeping staircase that once was an elegant town house was reduced to piles of lumber, only to be resurrected in 1988 at 5720 Chandler. "A 1949 ranch-style home is remade into a French country manor", was the newspaper headline when Jim and Cherie Flores transformed the Clint and

Molly Pierson house at 6326 Highland Road on what Cherie called "the prettiest piece of land right in the heart of town". Complete with a formal European garden, the 20-acre estate between Highland and Burbank is now the home of LSU Coach Nick Saban. And in the way of lavish mansions, just up from them on Highland is the 'antebellum-style' Wright Adams home of Mike Wampold (with the original square columns changed to round columns – quite an engineering fete!) featured in a George C. Scott Jr. film.

III

There has always been an educational connection and many residents of University Acres, past and present, were faculty members of LSU that underscores the well-chosen name for the subdivision here. Even in 1902 the Parish School Board recorded that "Mrs. Mary Caroline McConnell generously donated one half acre on Highland Road in the Sixth Ward for school purposes". Highland School goes back over one hundred years and we turn again to the reminiscences of Gertrude McConnell Preston who gave us a picture of the first Highland School.

> "The school was built by those families who had children of school age and I assume they financed it jointly – the Knoxes, the Hergets, Delavilles, Hewes, Williams, Dukes and McConnells. The school was located on Highland Road close by the McConnell House. It was a simple one-room wooden structure with a narrow porch in front. We had no proper school desks but wooden benches with some sort of desk arrangement on which to write. To the left side on entering there was a shelf which held a bucket of drinking water and a

Moved to 5720 Chandler Dr. from N.6th Street, Baton Rouge c.1894 -Residence of the Hines family.

6326 Highland Road –
The Pierson house in the 1960's

With later remodeling, now the Saban's residence

community dipper. (The water was drawn from a well on the Childress property.) We must have had a wood stove of some kind but I don't recall it. There was a desk for the teacher and a blackboard across the back wall. I remember that we had a pitifully few books in our embryonic library! The year would be about 1902. I was not quite of school age but was sent anyway so as to make up the number required to secure permission from the Parish School Board to open a school – there had to be fifteen pupils. The teachers always stayed with us at the house. Our first teacher was Miss Lela Garig of Baton Rouge; the next two were Misses Belle and Cora King of Jackson; the last was Miss Fanny Robertson from West Baton Rouge."

The school continued until 1912 with Miss Blanche Capedeville and Mrs. Emily Kleinpeter as teachers. One who did not board with the McConnells remembered how considerate they were to her and would send heated bricks for her feet on the cold ride back by horse and buggy into town. One spot near the current campus was called "Halls Bottom" because the mud was so deep at certain low spots. The young teachers had to drive four or five miles by horse and buggy to the schoolhouse. The children would come in buggies too, or walk if the weather was fine!

In 1912 the school was moved further out on Highland Road, where Staring Lane intersects – more accessible to Perkins Road which was originally called Middle Highland Road, and "Miss Myrtie" Polizotto first taught, then was made Principal. In 1921 Highland School made a further move in order to consolidate Manchac, Morgan and Highland plantation schools. It was comprised at first of three rooms, in which a staff of three teachers (including the principal) taught nine grades. The spot that was chosen was about one mile north, still on Highland Road, across from Triches' store, now the Frameworks Gallery. It was an historic Civil War spot and according to author Powell Casey, was a Federal encampment with Union forces camped there. Another source claims it had been a breastworks thrown up by the Confederate Army with a cannon to protect the vital Highland Road and surrounding areas and although it saw no fighting, it was a treasure-trove for bullets, coins, buttons and such. By 1939 there were seven rooms, seven teachers and only eight grades. Bill Stracener recalls that the pupils were forbidden to cross Highland Road but with the teacher on duty distracted by one of the older girls, the boys could run across to get RC's and moon pies at recess. The school had a flagpole in a circular driveway and now boasted several rooms, a narrow front porch, a multi-holed outhouse, and two school horse-drawn covered wagons for transporting the children. One pupil, Joe Materiste, remembered the day when the horses ran away and the pupils were bouncing around as the substitute driver worked to gain control. Later on, Mrs. Weisgerber was the driver of the motorized bus for many years. One day when the heater broke in the school, Mrs. Myrtie enterprisingly had Mrs. Kennedy take the children for a picnic to Chatsworth Plantation which was a few miles away, rather than have them sitting in cold rooms. Shortly after this the plantation home burned down.

IV

In the late thirties, towards the end of the Great Depression, plans were drawn up for Highland Elementary School which would have eight grades, but in accordance with the findings of the Peabody survey, the two upper grades were discontinued, and

"Old" Highland School c.1930's, 8500 Block across from old Triche's Store.

"New" Highland School, 1941.

HIGHLAND GRAMMAR SCHOL
Baton Rouge, Louisiana

"THEN" and "NOW"

Miss Myrtie, Principal

Miss Geraldine Wall, Principal

Highland became the six-grade elementary school which it remains today. In 1940, the doors opened on a school set in eight acres which was to become famous for many "Firsts", many awards, and many innovative programs that would classify it in the top of its league because of the talented and hard working Principal Mrs. Myrtie Picou Polizotto who taught for thirty-three years. The curriculum focused attention on the arts – speech, art, music and other creative activities. The Parish had had art and music supervisors and interested and talented parents assisted the teachers in these programs. Betty Bollinger remembers that every year each class learned a different dance for the May Day Festival: "My favorite was when we did the minuet and wore such beautiful costumes. My friend Conway Gaston had to dress like a boy because we had more girls than boys in the class. I always felt sad for her when I looked at the class photo, because she didn't have one of those beautiful dresses that we wore for costumes. Fifty years later, when Conway and I looked at the minuet photo together, she told me that it had been a special day for her, because she got to be a boy!" Betty recalls Miss Myrtie: "This tiny woman seemed incredibly wise to me. With her hair pulled back in a little bun, she had eyes that sparkled brightly from behind her wire-rimmed glasses. Garnering utmost respect from parents, she clearly was a dedicated educator with a gentle soul and kind heart, but a stern disciplinarian who commanded from us our best. Miss Myrtie always visited each class on Fridays to call out the words on the spelling test. Great emphasis was placed on spelling, grammar and writing". Bill Stracener, in retrospect, feels he got the greatest start since she was his 1st, 2nd and 3rd Grade teacher "by default" and she was very demanding. But as a child, he always hoped to get an "easier" teacher. One ruse she had was to give a pupil a book – "I don't know what grade this is for, would you read it and tell me what you think?" Ora, Mrs. W. L. Childress wrote: "Miss Myrtie had been reared on a plantation and trained in the Normal School for Teachers at Natchitoches, continuing her education at LSU where she received her Master's degree. Her ideals were high, her judgment sound and her ambition for Highland School knew no bounds. Her ability for work and inspiring others was prodigious. She attracted able and loyal helpers." Many students were to become teachers in the school system and several principals and school administrators began their teaching careers under the legendary "Miss Myrtie" including Lillian Kennedy, Eugenia Tucker, Lillie May Taylor, Mona Terry, Ruby Babin, C. G. McGehee, and both Emily Lerner and Dot Kleinpeter Turner went to the old and new Highland School and taught there later. Eleanor Vignes Roberts now lives at St. James Place and one of her students remembers when she called out one day, "Pandemonium" which he thought was a cute way to get the class to come to order. Mrs. Roberts remembers Miss Myrtie fondly and as being "a great principal".

Geraldine Wall followed Miss Myrtie, who retired after thirty-three illustrious years, and she was a lovely, vivacious principal, wrote Ava Ulmer, and would often wear a flower in her reddish hair. She was related to Dr. Bill Wall on Sunset Blvd. There are many teachers who remember Miss Wall fondly and are remembered fondly themselves: Earline Nolan, Edith Babin, Violet Stracener, Emily Elliott, Louise Willett, Ruth Efferson, Barbara Hagood, Geneva Bateman, Jean Grenchik, Myra Lee, Joy Johnson, Mary Lou Loudon, Rosalind Fagan, Diane Jordan, Jerry Scallan, Eloise Landry, and others mentioned elsewhere. The neighborhood was home to many who taught or were on the staff at Highland. Edna West's father had a general store in

Teachers: Mrs.Draper, Mrs.Worley, Mrs.Nolan, Mr.Jumenville, Mrs.Willett, Mrs.Loudon, Mr.Leitsner, Mrs.Glasgow, Mrs.Childress, Mrs.Landry, Mrs.Babin, Mrs.Turner, Miss Stracener

Teachers' Art Class: Front: Mrs.Richardson, Mrs.Turner, Mrs.Hines, Mrs.Loudon, Mrs.West
2nd Row: Mrs.Willett, Mrs.Scriber, Mrs.Jordan, -, -, Miss Wall, Mrs.Emily L.Willett
3rd Row: Miss Stracener, Mrs.Childress, -. Mrs.Ada Ulmer, Art Supvsr., Mrs.Glasgow, Mrs.Roberts, Mrs.Draper

JANITOR AND MAIDS
Left to right: Jessie Robinson, Wilbert Butler, Mary Butler.

HIGHLAND SCHOOL FACULTY

Back row: Mr. Gerard Scallan, Miss Geraldine Wall, Mrs. Garnet Glasgow, Mrs. Sarah Parsons, Mrs. Louise Willett. Middle row: Mrs. Eleanor Roberts, Miss Violet Stracener, Mrs. Edith Draper, Mrs. Elaine Scriber, Mrs. Ruby Babin. Front row: Mrs. Mary Lou Loudon, Mrs. Doris Turner, Mrs. Earleene Nolan, Mrs. Betsy Shea, Mrs. Diane Jordan, Mrs. Ora Childress.

Anadarco, Oklahoma and traded with the Indians. Edna inherited a superb collection of Indian artifacts and introduced these ethnic interests of Spanish and Indian lore to her students. Virginia Worley said of Miss Wall that she taught her so much about teaching and life, and her own memories of Highland School are many: she had arranged to have a garden dug for her class and on that day a mule stuck his head in her window and a voice outside called out, "Where do you want the garden?" The children loved that! Virginia and Earline Nolan wrote a cookbook to raise money to buy fans for their schoolrooms before air-conditioning. They also took charge of a 2nd Grade outing to the New Orleans Zoo by train and bus which was an exciting event with many mothers participating. (Virginia Worley's son David was accepted as a counselor at the Grand Canyon National Park when Leslie Glasgow was Asst. Secretary of the Interior and said what a great learning experience it was for David.) A picture in an old newspaper has some of the teachers being instructed in the art of potting by Ava Ulmer. Maxine Richardson was one, and still has the pot that was pictured. She recalls that Geraldine Wall was so compassionate and understanding and also that she was a great storyteller and adored reading "How Come Christmas" and the Uncle Remus stories.

Everyone remembers the janitor, Wilbur. June Lank recalls, "Our son Bobby used to tell us that he was going over to help Wilbur". Wilbur was more than a janitor, he was a helper and friend to all the children and such a part of the school life for over twenty years. He loved to sit on a bench and tell stories to the children. Wilbur and his wife Mary made an indelible mark forever at Highland School – the story goes that one of the children was heard to wonder who was more important – Miss Wall or Wilbert!

By this time, University Acres was well settled and children of more than one generation have walked to this local school. (Betty Bollinger was envious of those who rode the school bus and she said it was a special treat to go home with someone on the bus, or ride to the symphony on Saturday mornings three times a year.) Elisabeth Heard Wilton was taught 1st Grade by Mrs. Babin in the old school, and years later Mrs. Babin taught her daughter Charlotte 1st Grade at the new school. She remembered the time a man came to the school with a monkey to entertain the children and he asked for a volunteer for a banana-eating contest with the monkey. Her brother Tommy Heard volunteered and to her embarrassment, beat the monkey! How well does one remember school days! Little John Claitor, however, decided that 1st Grade school was not for him and he started to walk home. As his father Bob tells it, the teacher ran after him and persuaded him to give it another try! Barbara Babin Holden recalls when she was about eight, visiting her Uncle Wick Babin and family on Menlo and the glare of the gas flares burning on the Harry Nelson property. Her Aunt Ruby taught 1st Grade and Barbara loved the little chairs and tables and pretty blue flooring in her aunt's classroom decorated with alphabet and numerals. She also remembered the lovely Christmas parties at the Hawkins' home and the block parties at the Kimblers' on July 4th and Memorial Day. Jo Lynn LeJeune Caffery's schoolgirl memories include the violin lessons given through the school system by Gwen Sawyer. "At Christmas in the 6th grade we had a concert. How thrilling to come to school at night, and dress in robes and paper collars in a bright and messy classroom then stand on those risers on stage and sing! We sang old Christmas favorites but the one I remember is "Let there be Peace on Earth". Today when I sing this in church I think back to that night. . . . A

HIGHLAND SCHOOL CHOIR

Mrs. Pearl Orton, Director

SIXTH GRADE FOLK DANCING CLASS

An active P.T.A: Front: Eleanor Cole, Janette McGuire, Gladys Black, Dot Dyer, Hazel Peters, Julia Hawkins. Rear: --, Mrs. Rupp, Mrs. Allen, Mrs. Hammatt

Nickey Bertrand, Josie Allen, Frances Harvey, Nanette Kirby, Lou Lastrapes, Josie Ballinger, Pat Hines, Jane Bayce, Julia Marks, Ida Hammatt.

Highland School P.T.A. members who assisted with the Senior Banquet, 1956:

Mrs. W. J. Evans, Mrs. Moss M. Bannerman, Mrs. George K. Floro, Mrs. Jordan G. Lee, Mrs. Carlos G. Spaht, Mrs. Robert E. Wood, Mrs. Clarence C. Harvey, Mr. Malcolm Bollinger, Mrs. J. A. Higgins, Mrs. Gordon C. Allen, Mrs. Donald G. Pipes.

talk given in the auditorium by Coach Nolan made a great impression on me. It was against smoking and chewing tobacco. . . ..". Barbara remembered the wonderful books she got from Mrs. Katherine Martin, the librarian, and the first time girls ever were allowed to wear pants to school (hers were gold-colored jeans), and the back of the playground where the huge pine trees were where she and her friend would dig in the cool sand beneath them and on one occasion, so lost in play that they hadn't heard the bell and looked up to find themselves quite alone. And then there was the school carnival and she had her fortune told in the gypsy's tent and by good fortune stepped out of the tent and found a roll of tickets on the ground and got to play even more.

Highland School had an exalted reputation in the Parish school system! Pat Evans, "Miss Pat", a noted television personality on "Romper Room" created a play for Highland School of neighborhood adults playing the parts of children. Dr. Moss Bannerman and Elwood Wright in their children's getup almost "stole the show". Roy and Willie Mae Odom were among the first settlers and were so important to the Acres in the early years. She was a guiding light in the P.T.A. as well as being President of the Civic Association many times, and Roy (Pop Winkle from his radio show) would print up invitations and announcements for the Acres events. A 1950's school report stated that the Highland P.T.A. was one of the most cooperative in the Parish, giving intelligent consideration to all problems and supporting all school issues enthusiastically! This standard continues to this day. Carolyn Cavanaugh on Dubois is the organizer of one of the most successful 'Reading Friend' programs in the local school system and many of her volunteers live in the Acres. Many remember the pleasure they got from the Bookmobile. Betty Bollinger writes: "Every Wednesday morning in the summer was Bookmobile Day. All kids rode their bikes to Highland school, where the bookmobile was parked. I loved the bookmobile." One of the librarians was the sister of Nanette Kirby of the Acres which made it special.

Bob and Pat Hines with their family on Chandler are a typical great addition to the neighborhood. Bob did Scout work and Pat was the beloved secretary of Highland School for years and now a granddaughter Laura Burgess lives in their family home. One day in the grocery store, a child who had been looking at her finally came up to her with her mother and said, "Miss Wall is our Principal and this lady is the Vice Principal" – Pat thought that was delightful. Pat Hines' successor as secretary was Sara Powell on Chandler. She remembers visiting Diane Hitt and riding her bicycle as a child around the tree on Chandler and deciding then and there that that was where she wanted to live, and she got her wish. (Bill Stracener remembers that only once in his years of delivering papers on his bike on the gravel road did he accomplish the whole route "without hands" – that tree on Chandler had to be negotiated hands-on much to his boyish annoyance.) Clayton and Bonny Mahaffey could always be counted on to help. They had five sons and generously "adopted" five of the live oaks at the school, one for each son who went to school there. Dr. Joe Campbell of the Agricultural Economics Department at LSU, his wife Helen and family are fondly remembered. During the war years when 'Life' Magazine ran a teacher's beauty contest, students of Helen, when she was teaching in Ithaca, New York, submitted her photograph and she was one of the chosen.

A most lovable and innovative teacher both at the old Highland School and new school was Mrs. Childress. She did so many special things to keep a child's interest.

A scene from "The Pageant of the Seasons"

Spring 1955

Ladies assisting Mrs. Rupp:
Mrs. McKean, Mrs. Harris, Mrs. Rupp,
-, Miss Myrtie, Mrs. Odom, - .

"Pop Winkle" – Roy Odom

P.T.A. On Stage! Dr. Moss Bannerman with Miss Pat of Romper Room.

Elwood Wright and Dr. Bannerman take a back seat with the rest of the "class".

She had a "five-minute club" for those who could say their multiplication tables in that time – and many did, which was a mark of distinction – as was her "club" for those who could recite the Gettysburg Address. How many recall that they strove to be club members! (Betty Bollinger was president of those clubs by virtue of being the first in 4th grade to memorize each.) Mrs. Childress knew the Governor's wife, Mrs. Blanche Long, and got the class invited for tea to the Governor's mansion. She did not tell the principal beforehand because she was afraid she might not get permission. Mrs. Ida Hammatt drove the school bus to that lovely affair. Mrs. Childress also got T. Harry Williams to address her class – nothing was too good for them. (When she first bobbed her hair, the School Superintendent, Mr. Hatcher, called her a 'flapper'). Their oldest son Michael went to Annapolis and roomed with Bob Claitor who later moved into the old McConnell home. They remained firm friends for life and sister Ruth later married an Acres settler, John Murray, and the young couple settled behind his parents' house on Menlo. Over the years Ruth had wanted Jackie Richard's recipe for white fruit cake and in researching history, Jackie's daughter has come up with the recipe and here it is:

WHITE FRUIT CAKE

1 lb. Butter
1 lb. Sugar
1 lb. Flour
1 lb. Candied Cherries
1 lb. White Raisins
1 lb. Candied Pineapple

2 lb. Pecans
12 Egg Whites
8 oz. Citron (finely chopped)
1 pkt. Grated Coconut
4 oz. Whiskey
- Bake at 275 degrees

We heard from a beloved Third grade teacher, Edie Draper, well remembered for her reading of "The Little House on the Prairie" who still has the note from the precocious President of her 3rd grade class one year which read, "Dear Mrs. Draper, if you weren't married to Mr. Draper, we could sure have a good time. Love, Pres." She has many memories, as you may imagine. One had to do with the neighborhood monkey that belonged to the Hawkins'. This monkey was a source of amusement to the Acres, but one day it got into the boys' bathroom and one of her students came screaming back to her that a monkey was there: "It didn't take too long for me to solve the mystery – a call to Julia brought its owner to the rescue". Another story has to do with "Jigs". "He was a wire-haired terrier belonging to Oscar Barnes that followed him to school every day, got in line with him and marched right into the classroom. He would settle himself under the desk and take a nap. The only time he budged was if his master went up to the blackboard – he went too, placing his front paws on the chalk ledge and returning to the desk again. "One day, school board members visited. Jigs was at the blackboard with his master. I thought, "Oh, Oh"! The only comment was, "It's wonderful that the neighborhood dogs are being educated too". I have so many fond memories of Highland School". Needless to say, family dogs play a part in many reminiscences. At the end of the 4th Grade school year when Pam Woodin's red Irish setter "Rebel" had come to school every day and sat under her desk, it got a "Perfect Attendance" certificate. It was the respective dogs of Maria Standifer and Barbara Hagood that introduced them to each other. Boots McArdle recalls the family being locked out of the house and the neighbor's dog not taking kindly to the babysitter climbing through their bathroom window. The Acres was a wonderful place for dogs!

Betty Bollinger liked babysitting when she was in high school: "I was paid 50 cents an hour, no matter how many children. The rate never changed. My biggest

The playground of Highland School then and now.

Memorial magnolias shown on the left.

was baby-sitting the McArdle boys who lived in the Circle – five red-headed boys who were *all* boys! Years later I met Frankie, and he asked if I remembered him. "I was the good one!" he reminded me".

The Hagoods bought Sarah and Ben Downing II's house at 736 Dubois and Sarah says how much she loved the Acres – "The children could ride their bikes and play all over the neighborhood without you worrying". Betty Bollinger, who contributed much to this memoir, put it very well: "I lived in University Acres at a time when the word *security* meant your father had the same job all his life, and one thought nothing about burglar bars and alarm systems. In fact, the car keys never left the ignition and the doors to our home were never locked! The boundaries of our world were Nelson (which at that time was the city limit for south Baton Rouge), Chandler, Dubois and Highland Road. We children wandered the neighborhood at will. Someone's mother was within shouting distance if help were needed. Almost every home had a mother available all day, few families had more than one car and the windows and doors of our non-air-conditioned homes were always open. When my brother Jim was five years old he pulled the top of his finger off in a folding chair at the Kirbys' home. He came screaming across the street and my mother drove him to the hospital immediately. Dr. Levy asked where the finger was and Nanette Kirby, on hearing the screams and seeing the blood had had the good sense to wrap the finger and put it on ice which she took to the hospital and it was sewn back on – thanks to Nan and Dr. Levy. This is the kind of watchful eye that was always present in University Acres in the 50's." And yes, the Acres was a wonderful place for children, in this era before television dampened their imagination!

V

The Hawkins' children put on a circus in the summer for many years and would spend their summers making preparations for the great day with streamers, flags and posters.   Lots of costumes, balloons, funny stunts, popcorn and peanuts, a horse, trained dog and monkey, gymnastics – well over one hundred attended and the day before the Big Circus Day, participants made up the Parade of horses, bikes, go-carts and their Model A Ford – Jerry Hickel, Pattie West, Marcia Carter, Brian Calvit, Scott and Wallie Nesbitt, Rickey and Allen Jackson as well as Lad, Warren, Margaret and Jugie Hawkins were members of the cast and have wonderful memories of those days. A trip to Goudchaux's on Main Street was fondly remembered by the Navratil children who got a nickel for every A on their report card at the end of the school year, and the rambunctious Santa Claus with his Ho, Ho, Ho at Christmas time.   Goudchaux's was a family experience in those days – it made history for having the highest sales per sq. ft. in the U.S.A.   The side of the Navratil house often resembled a workshop (the neighbors were very tolerant) as the boys built transportation out of a wrecked car, or in the case of Philip with James Brown from Sunset, built from plywood sheets a 19 ft. Pelican class sailboat from plans Philip got from the school library.   The mast was laminated 1x4s with brass screws, and blue-painted, it was given a final coat of fiberglass resin.   Constance remembers turning over the living room to the job of sewing the sails and her Singer never quite recovered from the massive task.   Philip and James spent the whole summer earning money by painting houses and yard work to pay for the cost of the materials.   The Browns and the Navratils were present at the launching of the "Ariola" at Pensacola Beach. One summer Peter Navratil scavenged a large sheet of plywood from a trash pile outside Dr. West's house that started them on building a tree house. With John, Philip and James Brown, they made an A-frame construction complete with the electrical wiring done by Peter that was dubbed "The Tiltin' Hilton" and the concrete stair base is still in someone's yard in Woodstone.

For many summers, Nanette Kirby spent hours directing children's plays which were presented in her garage. "We all acted, built stage props, sold tickets, and built dreams" writes Betty Bollinger, "and summers in University Acres were the best! There were many girls close by – my family had three, the Hitts next door had two. The Woodins across the street had three, and the Murrays had two. We played canasta every day – today I have no idea how the game is played. And we'd spend endless hours collecting rocks and sorting them for sale on a card table in the Hitt driveway. When the day began to cool off in the evening we played croquet in our back yard, or played badminton at the Hitts, or played in the tree house or "camped" in our backyards. My brother Jim's friends practiced baseball in our backyard. My dad coached them, and Bob Nolan was the assistant coach. The Tasty Bakers started playing Little League ball together in 2nd grade and won the city championship every year, all the way through high school. Many of the boys continued to play together until after they were fifty years old and my parents went to all their games until the very end."

A great addition to the summer activities was the Highland School Summer Playground Program run by the Park & Recreation Commission in the early 60's with a supervisor. Many activities were planned: games, contests, picnics and refreshments.

"Box hockey was a big favorite" recalls Beulah Bolton. She continues, "Summer was great! We had a big back yard and set up a pole vaulting pit. Children came over and had track meets complete with stopwatches and competitions. All week long I would make and freeze Popsicles and on Saturday morning I would make doughnuts for them. The oldest son, Michael built a go-cart with a lawnmower engine and everybody had fun with that. We had a tree house in the back yard – far back – and the boys would take their pillows and a book out there for nap/rest time. Later on with the park at Menlo, my grandchildren have fond memories playing there on every visit and now I sometimes take the great-grandchildren there!!"

Mickey Jackson, Ruth Dillemuth, Sue Kimbler and Ruth Hyatt – the "Guava Street Coffee Gang" - started taking turns making coffee at 2 p.m. on week days. During the summer when the thirteen children were home they had a "rest period" from noon until 2 p.m. No child was allowed to disrupt his quiet reading activities or the mothers' break! As new families built homes on Guava, the moms took turns serving the coffee break – Helen Law, Lottie McGill, Joy Young, Sue Kimbler and June Lank joined the gang. In February of 1976 Ruth and Jim Hyatt started a Supper Club with much the same group.

There was the social ballroom dancing run by B.R.E.C. for 6th Grade students. Mary Elizabeth and Nelson Goings moved into the Acres in 1962 and they were asked to organize this at Highland School: "We had taught dancing 'in our youth' so with the approval of Miss Geraldine Wall and the School Board we paid a fee for the use of the lobby and janitorial services and met on Friday nights for an hour. There were about thirty in the class in each of the four years it was held and we taught them social etiquette and ballroom dancing which included fox-trot, waltz and jitterbug. A Christmas dance was held at the Woman's Clubhouse each year with refreshments but the end-of-schoolyear dance was at our home when we moved out furniture and rolled back the rugs. It was fun (if the waxing of the floors next day was not)!"

Julia Hawkins reminds us: "One of the most fabulous, famous and fun things of our neighborhood was the Great Halloween Carnival at Highland School which took place at Halloween. This activity went on for many years and was to the children like a World's Fair and State Fair rolled into one! Almost everyone who had children was involved, engineered by the P.T.A., the Room mothers and their committees, and the faculty as the big fund-raising event of the year. Local stores collaborated in donating goods and prizes. The school grounds were awash with booths brightly decorated in orange and black. There were games of skill, a fish pond, beanbag throws (Leo Bankston had painted the huge black cat that was used for many years), knock-down milk bottles, fortune tellers, but Betty Bollinger's favorite was the Spook House set up in Mrs. Babin's 1st grade room. "Unlike today's high-tech haunted houses, the biggest thrill was to get blindfolded and allow someone to lead our hands into a "bowl of eyeballs" (which I discovered later were merely peeled grapes) and across "a plate of brains" which I always knew were noodles." There were all kinds of sweets, candy, sticks of sugar cane, cotton candy, cupcakes and . . . cakes, all kinds. The cake walk where you might win a cake, and the "white elephant" stalls where someone's trash might be your treasure were always popular. All was purchased with tickets, bought at a booth at the entrance to the fair. Most dressed in costume which added to the fun, and the crowning event was Mrs. Rupp's Spaghetti Dinner at the cafeteria. Betty

Bollinger would help her father, who was the PTA president, to count the money after the dinner: "There I saw my first silver dollar. Daddy allowed me to purchase it with four quarters from my piggy bank, and I still have that silver dollar to remind me of the Highland School Halloween parties." What an exciting day for children and grown-ups alike! Julia goes on to say that Mary Jane Rupp was so much more than the school dietician and cafeteria manager – she was an inspiration for the neighborhood and President of the Civic Association many times. At school, she would provide coffee and biscuits as some little treat for the staff at morning recess and she also gave a Senior Banquet for the graduating 6th Graders and teachers. Her generosity of spirit, warmth and enthusiasm is recalled by all who knew her and her granddaughter, Janelle Earle and Mike her husband now live in her home at 220 Leeward. These acts of kindness permeate the memories conjured up by the residents.

A neighborhood coffee club had been started early in the war which added momentum to the Parent Teacher Association. Clarence Harvey, an engineer at Ethyl Corporation, and his wife Frances on Chandler were so helpful and Frances was President of the PTA at the time of integration, handling a delicate situation wisely with finesse. She was also a State officer of the PTA. It was the PTA who helped with the special trip of the choir to Birmingham and purchased a piano for Miss Cox, the choir teacher, which was known as Miss Cox's piano for years. Mary Jane Rupp was one who loved music and encouraged childrens' interest in music and to attend the matinee symphony concerts for the schools. The children participated – it was considered such an addition to their education. The PTA also stepped in, found funds and a sponsor, to provide the school with a canteen and help refurbish the auditorium. This auditorium

CARNIVAL TIME!

Mrs. Mary Jane Rupp
School Lunchroom Dietician,
As well as President of the
Acres Civic Association.

has accommodated some of the greatest names in the world of chamber music. The Baton Rouge Chamber Music Society was formed in 1963 and brought international guest ensembles to Baton Rouge, performing at Highland School.

VI

The Arts are well represented in the roster of Acres Residents. Professor of violin, Louis Ferrara lived on Dubois, Forest West, a renowned basso also on the LSU Music Faculty lived on Sunset Blvd and his wife Edna taught at Highland; Prof. Giles Gray of the Speech Department lived on Dubois and Prof. Guilbeau, Head of the Tiger Band lived on Highland Road. Sharon Matthews brings dance to the scene, as co-Artistic Director of the nationally recognized Baton Rouge Ballet Theatre, and her daughters are well-known actors. Both Sharon and her husband Bill grew up here and her mother, Nona Walker lives on Leeward Dr. John and Beth Dupaquier who maintain a piano studio at their residence on Chandler are famous for their Summer Jazz Fest that gathers aficionados from all over. When they were just starting, they inherited some students from Edna West who taught piano before teaching full-time; their first was Helen Reddy and "she was a joy to teach." Edna's son Jim and granddaughter Katie became pupils too. John remembers playing in the locally famous Big Band of Ovid Leonard who, with his wife Ruby, lived at 5875 Highland Road for many years. District Attorney Doug Moreau now makes this his home. Doug is the son of Al and Lillie Mae Moreau and is a former great LSU football player. He is one of the radio announcers for the football games. Richard and Jeannie Matheny are long time residents on Dubois and she is a fine artist. Constance Navratil soprano and actor, lives on Nelson Drive and was a classical music voice on Public Radio from its inception, for many years. Their neighbor, Malcolm Robinson is another well-known voice on radio. Our resident poet, Ava Haymon is a popular performer at the Baton Rouge Gallery, and an authentic bagpiper and member of the Caledonian Society is Stanley Masinter. Ava Ulmer at 704, was the Art Director for EBR Parish Schools and illustrated several books. Further down Nelson on 770, lived the legendary outdoorsman of television, the old Beachcomber, Bob Scearce. Jean deTarnowsky (cousin of Prof. George Pugh) is a past master in the art of patchworking and Thelma Berg is a well-known quilter. Her husband, Dr. Eugene Berg in the Chemistry Department at LSU is an avid orchid grower and instructs at the Orchid Society meetings. On Nelson Drive lives the photographer Sage, and across the street, Bill Stracener, whose paintings hang in important venues throughout the U.S.A.

Bill Stracener was born in 1928 on Nelson Drive, then Sycamore, and he has provided so much of the Acres lore. From the days when he was delivering the daily 24-page newspapers in the Acres with his brothers (he still has the book listing his route's customers) he recalls the families who lived on Highland Road at that time when it was still a wooded small road – C.L. and L.C. Learner, F.Polizzoto, J.C. Haase, W.N.Mitchell, W.A.Read, W. L. Childress, Dr.Guilbeau – on the corner of Nelson Drive, and a handful of residents near to Highland, those streets being gravel – Joe Richard , Pierre Becker, John Murray Sr. who also was an artist and served in the Army in the Panama Canal (Eva Murray was an Army nurse, having graduated from Touro's first Nursing Class): Harry Nelson who lived in the old McConnell home, and the Kreagers. Bill remembers that after heavy rain, the intersection of Menlo and Nelson

"Dead Man's Pond" at the end of Chandler Drive.

Artist Bill Stracener with pet goats.

The house in which Bill was born. Moved to adjoining Lot, 337 Nelson – Residence of the Annis family.

C. L. Stracener house: 250 Sycamore / 254 Nelson. Built 1926
Violet, Mrs.C.L.Stracener, Ivan, Mildred, Myrtle, -, -, -, Mr. C.L.Stracener

THEN and NOW

Sponsor Stanley Gross (L),   Coach Harry Hathaway (C),   Sponsor Leonard Gremillion (R)
Front Row: Joel Hindman, Steve Walker, Raymie Hathaway, Scott Haygood, Kerry Rhys, Gary Walker
2nd Row: Frank McArdle, Warren Brosset, Greg Dirksmire, James Teakel, Harry Richardson, Tim Johnson
Back Row: John McArdle, C.B. Annis, Drew Dicharry, Guy Mahaffey, Scott Nesbitt, Kelly Johnson

Christmas Choir Pageant
John Kent, past president of the University Acres Civic Assoc., 3rd from right.

always flooded with up to a foot of standing water – more childhood fun. His father had bought acreage on Nelson Drive and built across from his uncle, Bill's great-uncle, coincidentally, without either knowing about this. One of the oldest houses on Nelson, built in 1926, it was the largest, and needed to be, since Bill's uncle produced three sets of twins among his eight children. Bill recalls his childhood of exploring swamps and woods in the area – and "Dead Man's Pond", still at the end of Chandler Drive. Most of the football games and kite-flying was done on Thomas's property along Highland Road until Highland School was built and game activity shifted to the big school yard. Prewitt Nelson joins Bill in recollecting those days. Prewitt remembers that bikes got them around, often to the LSU campus, sometimes all the way to downtown: "Sandlot football games in a 3-team league were usually contested on the Highland School athletic fields. The other teams, one from University Hills and the other a bunch of ringers from all over, lobbied for neutral sites. The latter team called itself the "Mansion Team" because it had Jimmy and Billy Boyer, sons of Mrs. Sam Jones, wife of the governor. The big game of the series began after a bike brigade to LSU's baseball stadium and a tight squeeze through a locked gate, or over a barbed wire fence, depending on the girth of the player. After playing a couple of hours we were run out of there and found vacant grounds for the second half behind fraternity row off Dalrymple. Was there general agreement over any winner? Buddy Holden was our major ball carrier, Bill Stracener and Joe Richard were also backfield stalwarts and ends and the rest of us no-talent walk-ons played on the line. Equipment was sparse: some had helmets, some had tennis shoes, but that was about it, except maybe for a water bucket."

During WWII a number of Acres boys were in the Anzac Patrol of Boy Scout Troop 50 which was one of the most active and recognized in the Istrouma Area Council – Prewitt Nelson, Edward Parker, Alfred 'Buddy' Holden, Joe and Jack Richard, Lou DeGeneres, Eddie Gray, John Kent – and Bill Stracener drew the Anzac soldier in India ink on the shoulder patch of each member. Mrs. Parker sewed together tents of muslin which were then dipped in paraffin as waterproofing so that the scouts had their own tents for camping. They met in a hut by the LSU stadium and Clifton Smith was the wonderful scout leader until he got drafted. Bill remembers that Polizzotto's Nursery was situated on land which is now the University Baptist Church that provided much of the plantings for the neighborhood and the Church had even set a week-end when neighbors could dig up plants for themselves cheaply. We are indebted to Prewitt Nelson and Bill Stracener for their reminiscences. These days, Bill derives much pleasure from families enjoying his pet goats that forage peacefully in the backs of Nelson and Menlo across from the famous Dutch barn, torn down in 2002. It is nice to think that the old barn on 6262 Menlo has been replaced by an old home; the Reed house was moved from Highland to this location by Don and Jamie Carruth and fits the scene perfectly.

VII

Luminaries of other professions abound, and not all can be listed because of space but there is a strong connection with the University. Former President Martin Woodin, former Chancellor of the Law School Winston Day and former Chancellor of UNO Homer Hitt have made their homes here, as well as President of LSU John

The old barn on the corner of Nelson and Menlo, torn down in 2002.

Carruth Residence-6262 Menlo: the old Reed house moved from Highland Road to the site of the old barn.

Hunter, Chancellor of the Agricultural Center Norman Efferson and LSU Chancellor Paul Murrill. Paul and Nancy moved to Sunset Blvd. in 1972 and he later was Vice President of Ethyl and Chairman of the Board of Gulf State Utilities; members of University Baptist Church, Nancy was their first woman deacon – she is also an avid and knowledgeable collector of Staffordshire and porcelains. Dr. T. Harry Williams settled at 353 Nelson Drive in a bungalow built in 1927 that he purchased from Ben Carroll with additions made by A. Hays Town after his marriage to Estelle. So popular were his history courses that students queued to sign-up and the last lecture he gave (to 400 seated in the auditorium) was filmed for posterity. His book "Huey Long" won a coveted Pulitzer prize as did his "Lincoln and his Generals". His neighbor Alma Pellerin remembers getting him to autograph his books for her over the backyard fence which he signed, "To my burned out friend" since she had had a fire! Prize possessions of that famous Civil War buff were the two hand stitched tapestries above his fireplace depicting a Confederate and a Union soldier. Drew and Robin Patty have retained the original bungalow, which was named "The Lincoln House" by T. Harry and where he worked on his historical writings.

One of the sayings around LSU was that if you wanted to be a Boyd Professor, you had better move to Nelson Drive! In the 60's there were four: T. Harry Williams in History, Phil West in Chemistry, Grover Murray in Geology, and George Lowery in Ornithology. On Leeward Drive lived Dr. Madison B. Sturgis, the 'Whose Who in the USA' Agronomy Professor. Ernst "Fritz" Maser taught Aeronautical Engineering at LSU. He had been a German Ace pilot from WWI and knew Baron von Richthofen, the "Red Baron". He had been a classmate of Willie Messerschmidt and during the war, would be called to Washington to give advice on the designs of the latest German planes. He is credited with sending out many fine students, including two named in the Louisiana Engineering Hall of Distinction. Boris Navratil remembers meeting Prof. Maser at a gathering of German-speaking students at Maser's home at 699 Nelson Dr.

George Kirby and his wife Nan lived on Leeward. Nanette hosted many picnics and parties for the Association and continued to do so even after they moved to Highland Road and insisted on being kept as a member of University Acres. Prof. Kirby attracted attention on receiving his doctorate at the astounding age of twenty-four and went on to blaze trails in world negotiations as a director of Texas Eastern Pipelines. He was LSU Alumnus of the Year in 1978. Dr. Albert Meier and Arlene live on Chandler and he and a colleague have received patents on their research in the field of metabolism, receiving a Master Research Award from LSU.

Mention has been made of LSU Boyd Professors, LSU's highest distinction: renowned Chemistry Professor Dr. Philip West built his home on Nelson in 1940 and held the Presidency of the International Chemistry Association. An authority on air pollution, he tested air quality while flying his plane – and took aerial photos of our wooded sub-division. Another Boyd Professor Dr. Bill Patrick, world specialist of Wetlands and his wife Dr.Ruth, a noted nutritionist (known for wearing her signature hibiscus) who was with the Pennington Biomedical Research Center, bought the Carlos Spaht house at 888 Dubois; their son, Dr. Billy Patrick and his family make their home on Chandler. Boyd Prof. Al Bertrand and his wife Nickie who lived on Chandler were responsible for Leo Bankston learning about a lot that was for sale and settling his family in the Acres in 1955. (Our thanks to Leo who was with the Water Works

Eglin Residence-785 Leeward: the Sturgis house.

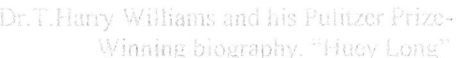

Dr. T. Harry Williams and his Pulitzer Prize-Winning biography, "Huey Long"

His work cottage "The Lincoln House" on 353 Nelson Dr.

Department and arranged for a water supply to the Blvd. area of the Acres sign on Sunset.) Dr. A.N. Yiannopoulos, world authority on Admiralty Law lives on Sunset and has been editor of the Louisiana Civil Code for a number of years. Richard and Louise Wiggins were both journalists, he at LSU and Louise was a free-lance. Theirs was a house on Dubois that had an elevator! Prominent judges, lawyers, doctors, dentists, publishers (in addition to the Claitor family, Bobby and Billy Prescott have the Co-op Bookstore) grace the area.

There are so many interesting people including the current NFL Coach of the Year champion Nick Saban who coached the LSU National Champions football team of '03 and lives on Highland Road, and our late, great Charlie McClendon. Charles and Dorothy Faye moved to 5930 Menlo in 1962. He was assistant coach with Coach Dietzel's first National Champion team. He took over as Head Football Coach at LSU for eighteen years – "the winningest coach ever". He set up a 'Charles McClendon Scholarship Foundation' to aid family members of his ex-football players. This gives the measure of the man, and he and Dorothy Faye were treasured Acres people. Two sons, Lloyd and Barton, and nephew Dell Walker of Agnes and J. B. Frye, who was head of the Dairy Department, played football for LSU. The Acres "Grand Athlete" was Al Moreau. He held the world record in the 120 yd. High Hurdles in 1935 and was Head Track Coach at LSU from 1949 to 1963. He won seven championships in Southeast Conference competitions. His wife Lillie Mae was a Heck, from a family of musicians and at one Coffee Club meeting at their home those present got to sing from booklets she gave them – "Music by Heck". Theirs was a wonderful family. They had ten children and on their Golden wedding the children gave them a surprise Hawaiian

Party and tickets to Hawaii.   Then there were Jim Taylor, Green Bay Packer fullback and later a member of the New Orleans Saints, three LSU basketball players – Bobby Nolan, Benny McArdle and Jordy Hultburg, and LSU football player for Coach Dietzel on his National Championship team, Gus Kinchen, who is now Area Director of the Fellowship of Christian Athletes.   Gus's wife Toni was an LSU cheerleader along with another Acres "oldtimer" Bill Bankhead.   Bill moved with his wife, Mary Ann, and mother to Sunset Blvd. behind his uncle who had the Caldwell house.   His family had run the store on the corner of McDonald and Highland Road that served the Acres so conveniently and when he graduated he was the Director of the Pete Maravitch Assembly Center until he moved to Colorado to take over the training camp for the U.S. Olympics Team.   On his return to Baton Rouge he became head of the National Senior Olympics.   Senior Olympians – Thelma McDowell, J.B. Frye, Bill Patrick, Ned Hickel, Julia Hawkins and Bill Stracener add to the scoreboard.   On Highland Road lived the Richardson family, Dr. Roger Richardson Dean of the Engineering Faculty and his wife Cary.   Their famous son Hamilton of Tulane University won the NCAA Championships in 1952, 1953, 1954, and in 1958 the U.S. Open Tennis Doubles with Alex Almedo, and was in the USA Olympics Tennis Team that took him to Wimbledon. (His aunt, Maggie Dixon, was thankful to the Acres for the safe return of her myna bird that had escaped while she was moving.   When a strange bird was heard in the neighborhood, its owner was traced through a radio announcement and the myna bird was reunited with Maggie).

This 'famous' list is endless in an eighty-year coverage.   There are even one or two "infamous", such as the Jackson house at 5786 Highland Road embroiled in

6015 Highland Road – political scandals surrounded the Caldwell house.

5876 Highland Rd. – the Jackson house involved in political scandals.

political scandals before J.A. and Helen Rockhold became the owners. The Christmas Party was held there the year of the great freeze when City Park lake froze over and so did their pipes – no water but good spirits! The beautiful home of LSU Buildings Supervisor "Big George" Caldwell which adorned the corner lot on Sunset Blvd. and Highland Road was also built with materials stolen from the University that included gold bathroom fixtures. Even so, the Caldwell house was much lamented when torn down in 1998, sixty years after the Louisiana scandals which sent George Caldwell to federal prison. Harnett Kane called it "a mansion that put all of its neighbors to shame" and the former owners, Dr. Bankhead and his wife Maize, heard the news with great sorrow. She remembers hundreds of parties they had there. The Bankheads held a big barbecue for Gov. Jimmie Davis and a tea for Mrs. Earl Long when her husband became governor. "Practically every football game we had a party and sometimes a brunch the next morning. One year the Lady of the Lake Auxiliary had its silver tea at the home and it was the largest turnout in history – everybody wanted to see the house. For one party, floral designer Jim Sanchez cut a magnolia tree from the property and stood it in the lower entrance hall in a huge antique wooden wine cooler then wired hundreds of magnolias on the tree which reached to the ceiling of the entrance hall on the second level." The double curving exterior stairway lead to a wide second story veranda. On either side of the large entrance hall were the dining room, left, and the living room on the right. Three identical Waterford crystal chandeliers lit each of the rooms. Originally the rooms opened onto porches at the two front corners of the house; the Bankheads glassed in the porches to create a music room and a solarium. At the back of the entrance hall a circular interior stairway lead to the lower floor and the kitchen, breakfast room, master bedroom suite and famous playroom with horseshoe bar. Maize said, "When we first moved in, Steele Burden returned to see that the grounds were immaculate – every window in the entire house had a beautiful view!" James and Janet Pierson later became the owners until 1993.

VIII

No greater tribute to the natural beauty of University Acres can be made than citing it as the home of the late Boyd Professor Dr. George Lowrey, an internationally-known scholar who founded the LSU Museum of Natural Science who, with his protégé Dr. John O'Neill, have been described as the "poet laureates of the world of birds". Dr. Lowrey and his wife Jean with their two daughters bought property at the end of Nelson Drive reaching down to Bayou Duplantier and it was divided into three partnerships. Dr. Lowrey took the biggest amount of swamp area and made a bird sanctuary that he graciously allowed scout and school groups to visit for bird watching. His books on birds of Louisiana and mammals of Louisiana brought him great fame. He was President of the International Ornithological Society and many remember the artistic shadow-box with stuffed egret that graced the entrance to his home and was the replica of the design of the cover of his book "Birds of Louisiana". His neighbor partners were Dr. Hank and Sue Belle Werner who loved their wilderness place, and Dr. E. B. Roberts who was the neighborhood guru on snakes, frogs, lizards and butterflies. His lovely wife Eleanor taught at both the old and new Highland Schools.

Pride in the Acres was manifest from the beginning and owners soon began transforming the barren acreage with trees and shrubs they planted. Even the work of

Dr. George Lowery with covers of his famous books.

Daniel Residence-5877 Chandler Dr.: the Lowery house.

the great landscape architect and philanthropist, Steele Burden, is seen in the Acres. The beautiful old pine trees on every corner of the Acres, and probably some of the water oaks, were planted by Prewitt Nelson Sr., his daughter Olga tells us. In 1938, Fred Cochran of the LSU Horticulture Department planted the live oaks, dug up from the woods as seedlings, at 707 Dubois. Not long ago Constance Navratil received a visitor - Robert Folweiler, an elderly Bostonian gentleman - who remembered that when he was a child his father planted the four, now huge, tulip poplars in their yard and he was amazed how the years had transformed the neighborhood. Mike Cavanaugh was in his yard when a former owner, Jewel Allen, stopped by and nostalgically noted that they were still using her stove. Mike also met her daughter Linda with whose name they were all familiar as it was scratched into the curbside cement. . . . Teresa Lunsford also had a Mr. Hamilton who returned to view his old house – and sent a bouquet of flowers to her next day! Sentiment calls these former owners back to the Acres.

Lawrence and Jeanne George bought John Hunter's home at 6060 Chandler in 1958. He was editor of Louisiana Farm Bureau News for a while and later Editor of the Louisiana Experiment Station's Publications for years. Jeanne, the mother of eight, tells of meeting Irene Burbank one day who asked her how many children did they have. On being told, Irene's response was, "My dear, how do you do it?" Now more about the Burbanks. Current owners throughout the subdivision are enjoying the beautiful blossoms of ancient camellia trees of every variety, the legacy to the Acres of Bill Burbank with his wife Irene and son Bill Jr. Having retired from the insurance business, he devoted a great deal of time to his flowers, especially camellias. He would "jib" them to make the blooms grander and share his enthusiasm with many others, including, at that time, Grover Murray, Bob Hines, L.N. Stracener and Judge Carlos Spaht, bringing forth superb camelia trees with gorgeous blooms at new year all over the Acres. The myriad camellia bushes on the Spaht property were a wedding gift of her father to the first owner of the house.

It was a fifteen year old Taiwan cherry tree of Vivian Koonce on Chandler Drive back in the 60's that spurred Bill Burbank into thinking that perhaps here we could have a miniature Washington D.C. cherry show in springtime! Bill Burbank's thoughts turned into reality with the help of nurseryman Mr. Moles, and all along Highland Road, neighborhood chairmen of the University South Civic Association - College Town, University Hills, Plantation Trace, College Hill, Highland Hills, Magnolia Wood and further, as well as University Acres - began a "beautification". One hundred and twenty signed up to start. Julia Hawkins was named General Chairman and Mrs.Oscar Kimbler, Mrs. Vivian Koonce and Mrs. Edwin Sales worked with the Acres project. This project caught a lot of attention in the local press with each mass planting and in 1967, in commemoration of Arbor Day, Julia Hawkins, on behalf of the Association, accepted the Certificate of Appreciation from the City Beautification Commission. Over a thousand cherry trees grace the area and many others – Japanese magnolia, redbud and dogwood and in University Acres alone, 500 cherry trees were planted. In the early part of the year, how cheering it is to see the bright pink blossoms radiant against the gray backdrop of winter. When Bill was very ill, Mayor Woody Dumas visited him to tell him that the new road beyond Bayou Fountain would be named after him to honor all that he had accomplished, and University Acres dedicated a marker at

Mr. And Mrs. Bill Burbank
The "Unofficial Mayor" of University Acres.

Marker at the entrance to Sunset Blvd. honors William Burbank.

the entrance to the Acres, a quotation by Thomas Bailey Aldrich (1894-1975): "What is lovely never dies, It passes into other Loveliness, Stardust or seafoam, Flower or winged air."

Many Presidents of the Civic Association have served more than one time, including Mary Jane Rupp and Willie Mae Odom. Some dug in their heels and really made their mark and one such was Robert Rackley, who bought the old McKean home at 348 Leeward and lived there nineteen years. In 1969-70 curbs and gutters were installed and the road blacktopped, the cast-iron drain covers proudly displaying the name of the subdivision. A well-kept secret from their mother, the Navratil children crept through the new storm drain pipes all along Nelson through Chandler before they were put into service! (Why mothers go gray.) Looking back, Bob Rackley sees the paving of the streets, no matter how controversial it was at the time, as perhaps the lightning rod for the Acres. Momentum started to improve homes and yards, to plant more trees and landscape and without those paved street, the Acres would have fallen behind the development-curve in the Parish He saw to the monitoring and enforcing of City/building codes and subdivision restrictions through the Civic Association Board and overseeing rental property of children who had grown up and moved away, at a time when South Baton Rouge was evolving into the focal point of residential development in the Parish. He introduced the blue markers for fire hydrants, an idea later adopted by the City, and saw that the Directory was updated. In 1990 he inaugurated 'adopt a tree' at Highland School for work that needed to be done on many live oaks, and could often be found with a tractor, helping on a job or seeing that the Acres was spruced up. We owe a lot to Bob Rackley and his lovely wife Jeanette. An indispensable member of the board at that time was the secretary/treasurer Raye Seago who worked tirelessly. She and her husband John have lived in the Acres for twenty-five years. John Kent, who attended both the old and new Highland School and his wife Kitty have a long history with the Acres and was active as President and in the Neighborhood Watch system; Richard McDowell served several times, and their lovely home on Sunset is designed by Thelma's uncle, the renowned A. Hays Town. Ed Sale with his wife Sally, long-time residents have always been attentive, ready to give a coffee and help in any way; Jacques deTarnowsky, Mike McGaugh, Stephen Creed and others have been as keen to enrich our surroundings and enhance the quality of life in the Acres. The Neighborhood Watch was instigated and a children's park was added at Leeward Drive which has given much pleasure to the Acres families. In 1973 Sunset Boulevard median was landscaped and on the 50th Anniversary of University Acres a marker, designed by landscape architect Lad Hawkins, of heavy timbers that had come from the old Rosenfield's Store built in the 1880's, was installed with the name and date of 1923 and suitably landscaped. It was unveiled to a happy audience. In the write-up by Mary Champagne, she remarked that "it's a rather special neighborhood, special in the quality of its neighborliness". Julia Hawkins was the chairman, assisted by Leslie Glasgow, Gene Cretini, Dr. Eugene Berg, Mrs. William E. Smith, Mrs. Stanley W. Preston, Mrs. Cordell Haymon and Mrs. Gray Annis. This marker was renewed in replica by the good offices of Acre resident, architect Tommy Campbell. Nearby is the prettiest cherry tree in the Acres at the home of Dr. Bill and Gay Smith, who have been an inspiration to us all. Russell and Jeanie Washer are longtime residents on Sunset Blvd. and Russell, an outstanding architect, has done

CIVIC IMPROVEMENTS

Curbs and gutters, Cast-iron drain covers, a children's park for the Acres.

The unveiling of University Acres Marker on the 50th Anniversary.
Violet Stracener, Mrs. Myrtie Polizotto, Mrs. Ora Childress, Mr. and Mrs. Lerner.

University Acres Marker at the entrance to Sunset Blvd.

wonders with his house – they are also undoubtedly the tallest runners in the neighborhood! Dr. Robert Lank was head of the Veterinary Science Department and Associate Dean of the School of Veterinary Medicine at LSU. He and June lived first on Sunset and then moved to Guava and were always part of any Acres activity. Oscar Kimbler, who taught Petroleum Engineering at LSU, and Sue Kimbler who helped June Lank with the directory for years, were also supporters of the neighborhood. Their son Warren is an indispensable help and friend to many neighbors whose yards he keeps up.

The Association keeps an eye on the Acres' needs and the Beautification Chairman for many years has been Mag Wall who worked closely with Wanda Huh the landscape architect who designed the planting of the boulevard. Oscar Huh, Geologist at LSU and his wife Wanda are good neighbors – Bill Stracener chuckles when he remembers that their daughter Melanie and a friend were playing in his yard and he asked her name to which she replied, "Melanie". "Melanie who?" "Yes", was the reply. Mag handles the marker and seasonal requirements and helps in so many ways, and her daughter Sissy Stevens who lives on Chandler updated the directory with names and ages of children when she was President of the Association. Mag and her husband Dr. Bill Wall have been such an asset to the Acres for many years. By arrangement with Entergy, the neighborhood trees on Sunset Blvd. were trimmed, and in 2003 the project to mulch the fine oaks on the school grounds was implemented with the help of David Ridenour and Provco Tree Trimming.

Exercise "trimming" also has its place – (Mag Wall and her neighbors, including Catherine Maraist and Mignonne White, keep up quite a pace in their daily 7 a.m. walk in the Acres). There was a Highland School Parents vs. Southdowns School Parents basketball game for charity that many who participated will remember – Ginger Bourgois, Mary Helen LeJeune, Martha Boswell, Pat Hines, Josie Bollinger, Ruth Hyatt, Mickey Jackson, Julia Hawkins, Ruby Jolissaint, and Nanette Kirby was Cheer Leader. The men's team included Frank Hatcher, George Cardwell and the star was Bobby Nolan who played Varsity basketball at LSU, husband of our beloved teacher Earlene Nolan. Highland School won both the men's and women's games – hurrah! Years later in 1987 Don Phelps, Ben Charbonnier and Jim Wansley inaugurated the Fat Boy Five-K Race designed as a serious race with some fun. Tom Campbell is the official surveyor of the course and in 2003 there were 625 entries with such celebrity participation as Smiley Anders, Jordy Hultburg, Judge Mike McDonald, Brother Eldon Crifassi, Joe Macalusso, Mike Rhodes, Boots Garland, Richard Condon and Vincent Canatella. Inexpensive trophies are donated, with drawings of give-aways. The "official turn around person" for the one mile fun run is Acres resident June Lowe and her dogs in the lawn chair on Chandler. (This is an acknowledged "warm up" to the New Orleans Crescent City Classic 10K and takes place early in April.)

IX

There has been a coffee club in the Acres since the early 40's when young mothers would meet monthly, bring their knitting and provide a ready friendship. They were drawn together to help in Highland School activities and, during World War II when there were such restrictions on travel, the club provided a release from feeling isolated. At least they were able to take advantage of the Acres private bus service! Beverly Bateman Langlois of 645 Leeward, daughter of Bryant and Geneva Bateman –

The Annual "Fat Boy 5-K Race" that takes place each April.

Don DeGeneres Residence-850 Dubois Dr.: the home built by Mildred Dubois.

he taught Forestry at LSU and Geneva taught at Highland - tells us that the residents formed a corporation, pooled their gas ration coupons and bought a bus for the use of the members. Members took turns driving but 17-year old L.N.Stracener Jr. probably drove it most and the route was to the French House at LSU three times daily where it connected with the City bus which did not come out to the Acres. On 'V.E.Day', Mildred Dubois loaded the bus with every child she could find (Beverly, Emily and Evelyn Lerner Horton were three on that bus) and with numerous noisemakers - which included the bell that was kept across from the school on the circle to warn of danger - drove down Third Street making several cheering and screaming trips - some celebration!

Dubois Drive having been named after Mildred, she quite obviously played an historic role in Acres history! A Phi Beta Kappa from the University of Alabama, she was the "Girl Friday" to Harry and Prewitt Nelson when they moved here, being in charge of sales, aside from being a "Guardian Angel" to her many friends. The first woman to be elected to the City Council, all her life she added zest and joy to the Acres capers. She also brought her mother and sister to live in the Acres, building a home for them on Chandler. She had horses and at first had a stable across from her home, near to "Dead Man's Pond". She and her friend Fran Burns could be seen riding around the neighborhood in its early beginnings. She was a larger-than-life personality in the minds of all the children in her orbit.

And year after year the Coffee Club thrived! It was decided that an Acres Directory was needed and the task fell to June Lank with help from Helen Campbell, two stalwart workers for the Acres, to compile the first listing around 1956-57, by collecting information from mail boxes or by knocking on doors. Over the years, the project was enlarged until now there is a comprehensive 10-1/2 x 4 in. Directory of Residents that proudly states: "The purpose of the University Acres Civic Association is to promote the well-being of the subdivision, through physical improvements and social gatherings of the residents." Betty Bollinger recalls: "I remember the thrill when Mama was hostess for the University Acres Coffee Club that met on Thursdays. It was fun to help serve the coffee and refreshments to all these wonderful women. And wonderful, when I was grown, to return to visit my parents at 714 Leeward Drive and attend one of the coffees, or a summer picnic, or the neighborhood Christmas Party. It is indeed a credit to many wonderful people that this special neighborhood has a spirit of community that continues to thrive."

The Coffee Club to this day helps bond families in good times and bad and celebrated its 80th birthday at its 2003 Christmas Party. This is a resplendent annual event held every Yuletide in different homes of the neighborhood and is sponsored by the Civic Association. In early summer there is another 'gathering of the clan' with a picnic held in a designated host's garden. Mrs. Melva Bannerman had so many of these in her yard on Nelson that she was awarded a "fun" certificate. These parties might include children – and sometimes they didn't! Better Bollinger remembers – "the New Year's Eve parties where the children would "peek in" on the adults. And what a neighborhood party! Next door was Homer Hitt, across the street were the Woodins, Kirbys and Murrays. As adults, Mike Kirby and I often reflected on the collective mental power of our early mentors."

Malcolm and Josie Bollinger were a typical Acres family – big family, big lot and big heart. Anything they could do for the Acres they gladly did and now their son Billy and his family are living in the family home on Leeward.   Vern and Veva Dicharry lived on Leeward too for over fifty years, and Veva is such a part of the Acres. Elmer and Mary Heard and their son Ken were also long-time residents. Ken is a very fine artist and is also our Acres tree man! Jimmy Taylor and the Samahas on Chandler were such good friends that he still calls Violet to see that she is all right.   The Taylor house is now owned by Roy Coats whose mother, Doris, was a long-time teacher. A great friend to all was "Momee" Huckaby who lived with her daughter Mary Catherine Vanduzee on Chandler. For her hundredth birthday there was a tailgate party at the LSU/Tennessee football game – hundreds came and LSU won for her. What a way to celebrate a centennial! W.J. "Red" Evans and Mildred were an inspiration to us and so involved for the good of the Acres, holding the Christmas parties and Mildred as a close friend of Mary Jane Rupp, whatever the one couldn't manage, the other would take over and they worked together so enthusiastically. "Red" was an architect and bought Fritz Maser's house next door and connected it to his own at 701 Nelson for a number of years. It is now "detached" and his daughter Jane with husband Kevin Dyer live there now.   Helen and Jerry Law, long-time residents, and Blanche and Gene Cretini who so kindly hold picnics at their home with the welcome swimming pool in the summer further add to the atmosphere of co-operating in the Acres ventures and Helen and Blanche have done the Coffee Club great service.   Eleanor Burroughs on Chandler is always a reliable help in the Acres activities and it was also very nice when Laura

Nicholson and Rachel Fowler and another friend had a catering business and could help out when an emergency arose!

And the Acres residents have rallied in time of tragedy. L.N.Stracener, Jr. was in WWII and met and married an English bride, Maureen. Before their daughter was born he died in a motor scooter accident; Maureen bravely carried on and eventually was married to his good friend, the radio commentator Brooks Reed. Daughter Jennifer is one of the editors of the popular book 'Chicken Soup for the Soul'. There were several disasters from hurricanes and with Hurricane Andrew, one narrowly averted – Walter and Ann Legett on Nelson Drive had gone into the kitchen to make coffee early that stormy morning when a huge water oak fell on the other end of the house, demolishing the bedroom where they had just been sleeping. Neighbor Nita Ammon took them in, and they remember the outpouring of help during those early days. Dot Debosier lost a car at the same time when a tree fell on it. She has lived on Nelson for forty years, brought up her family, taught school, a great friend of Mildred Evans, and is quite a wonderful tour guide in her "retirement". Ken and Edna Wilson lamented the loss of a huge red oak during Hurrican Andrew that fell on their home and the house of Julius and Miriam Morris. Both are longstanding families in our midst and the Acres pulled together to help out after that particularly vicious hurricane.

Kimbro Owen and his family had lived at 707 Dubois. He was assistant to the Mayor Jesse Webb and both were killed in a plane crash – a great loss to Baton Rouge and to the Acres. And there was Willie Mae Odom's dreadful car accident where friends gathered to help and offer solace. Charlotte and Raymond Strawinsky with their daughter had a young Finnish student living with them on Menlo when a fire broke

Hurricane Andrew in 1992 uprooted trees throughout the neighborhood inflicting much damage.
 Above: the home of Mike and Caroline Cavanaugh at 744 Dubois Dr.
 Below: the home of Walter and Anne Legett at 766 Nelson Dr.

out and Prof. Strawinsky and the student perished and Charlotte was badly burned. This dreadful tragedy rallied the Acres to help in any way they could for many weeks as Charlotte slowly recovered. Drs. Richard and Holly Haymaker – he is a Physics professor at LSU and Holly is a doctor at EKL Hospital – bought the old Stracener home on Nelson Drive from Ruth Shoptaugh in 1976. The Peace Pole in their yard, with wording in Spanish, Japanese and English sends a message of harmony and peace among peoples and is a memorial of the tragic shooting in Baton Rouge of their Japanese exchange high school student, Yoshi Hattori one Halloween night, who was living with them and who was a dear friend of their son Webb. The magnolia trees at the back of Highland School were planted in memory of former Highland School students who were killed in World War II; one was the son of Mrs. Darden, Lyman F. Rhodes, a nephew of Miss Myrtie.

The Acres has a drawing power as can be seen by the number who have moved around and not away from the Acres. Dr. Harry Richardson, was head of the Nuclear Energy Department and with Maxine, in making their home in the Acres, they lived on Menlo, then built a splendid house on Highland which is now the Wampold home, and finally moved to 200 Leeward Drive – they knew the neighborhood well. Dorothy Preston Holden first moved in the early 40's to 684 Leeward Drive then watched over the building of 694 Sunset Blvd. and on moving in had the Acres Christmas party. Many have lived in more than one house in the Acres – Albert and Kathi Merey now live next door to her parents, Walt and Margie Whitehead and for years Albert was our own and special friend and mailman; June and Bob Lank, Grover and Nancy Murray, Alma and Don Chesson – they lived first on Leeward behind her parents' home, the

Barcelonas, then took over the family home on Highland Road – similarly, Robert and Ruth Woods moved to a larger home on Leeward with their large family, such a bright, eager family - Garnet and Les Glasgow who moved from the circle to 663 Sunset, Mr. and Mrs. L N. Stracener, the William Daniels the Fryes, Nan and George Kirby, Ruth Childress Murray and Bill Stracener. Gus and Toni Kinchen bought their home on Guava Drive from their son Todd. He had played football at LSU and went on to play with the Rams, the Broncos and it was with the Falcons that he went to the Super Bowl. John White carried his bride Mignonne over the threshold of their home on Menlo in 1959 and some years later, when they had actually bought another house and were on the point of moving, Mignonne knew she couldn't leave the Acres, the only home they've known – and they have never regretted their decision. John, a lawyer, was on the school board for six years and on the Planning and Zoning Commission, which gave us an ear to the network. Don and Jeune Pipes moved onto Boone Drive in the 50's and have added a lot to the group. Jeune was a longtime member of "Sweet Adelines" and was a great dancer. English professors at LSU, Jim and Edith Babin are long-time residents and enjoy the spectacular pine tree, amongst all the trees around, that dominates their front yard – Edith's father was a Hammatt of Mount Hope Plantation, part of the history of this area. Just down the street are Joe and Jackie Durrett who made their home here over thirty years ago. Families have stayed, even through second and third generation which brings to mind the family celebration Elizabeth DeGeneres treated her family to just a year before her death – all the family, about fifty or sixty of them gathered in Florida for the occasion. Her son Don lives in the Mildred Dubois house at 850 Dubois and another son Jim sent us the reminiscence that follows in the next section. Cookie Odom West and her family live in the family home on Nelson, and Mary Jane Rupp's granddaughter, Janelle with her husband Mike Earle live on Leeward Dr. Dr. Martin Woodin's daughter Pam and her husband Carl Fry live in the old home place.

X

No wonder that University Acres boasts of family connections and generations staying, returning, and remembering the close feeling of community. There are so many wonderful friends, too many to list, who have gone but are still remembered. World War II holds memories for some. Prewitt Nelson writes, "The war was the big event between early subdivision days and the really big postwar building boom. My first knowledge was from Jimmy and Johnny DeGeneres riding their bikes at top speed along Leeward and hollering "The Japs bombed our ships and we're going to war! It's on the radio". Prewitt continues, "For kids, the only formally recognized wartime duties were as aircraft spotters in the Aircraft Warning Service. We would bike down Highland to the Gardere intersection and climb a tower in the Hammatts' back pasture. We were told that our site and the one atop the capitol building guarded the third most important target there was. Baton Rouge ranked after Washington D.C. (governmental and military) and New York City (financial and commercial) because of the Ethyl plant next to Esso, the world's largest refinery. (At the beginning of the war Ethyl made all the tetraethyl lead additive for every single gallon of aviation gasoline used by the Allied War Effort). We must have done O.K. because not a single bomber got past us. Our frequent direct-line calls went to New Orleans, Atlanta or maybe to Washington to advise of six aspects of each sighting: number of planes, number of engines on each, altitude whether seen or heard, direction from our position and direction headed. Most were locally based fighters from Harding Field, but we studied silhouettes of German, Italian and Japanese aircraft to be safe. We received armbands for 20 hours of duty; Eddie Gray was the only one who reached 100 hours, earning a set of wings of some sort. As junior air-raid wardens we went around reminding householders to turn off their lights during blackouts. [A *major traffic accident* nearly occurred one dark night when Edward Parker and I brushed past each other on bikes on Chandler Drive.] Nighttime badminton on the DeGeneres' dirt court and swimming at Mildred Dubois' pool were the social centers. There was little at all of partying visible to that pre-college age – the really interesting lives of wartime youngsters came later; experiences added to the adventures that began in the Acres."

Jim DeGeneres also wrote a reminiscence that takes us back to the year 1941 when, almost six, he and his friends were playing football on Chandler when they were told that Pearl Harbor had been bombed. As children, they dug a victory garden, raised chickens, took part in scrap iron drives and were scared by the air raid warden and his blackout drills. The air raid bell was proudly paraded downtown when peace came! School memories include the half-pint glass bottles of milk sold in the auditorium (concrete floor) for a penny and the long lines for the water fountains – one for girls, one for boys.. ... Jim DeGeneres writes: "Who can forget the visits by Miss Myrtie to each classroom and reciting "The Grand Old Duke of York" with appropriate hand gestures; and the 5th grade school glee club's trip to Birmingham to sing at a music teacher's conference with Mrs. Cox. (To raise money, Jim shoveled horse manure for

The DeGeneres home, 1940 with Mary, Betty and Kitty DeGeneres

Lindsay Residence-5874 Chandler Dr.: the old DeGeneres house remodeled.

Mildred Dubois.) When I was in 7th Grade I delivered papers with my brothers for Mrs.Gilbeau, and Donald the youngest got University Acres. On my 15th birthday, which was the legal age for driving at the time, we bought a brand new Chevy truck for $1,546.32 – the three bicycle routes were combined to another large route and this was the birth of DeGeneres Bros and I'm sure many old timers remember our green pickup truck speeding through the Acres!

"Mildred Dubois and Fran Burns had a rather large swimming pool with sloping sides that had to be drained and cleaned every two weeks. Before improvements were made, a brave soul with rubber boots for gripping, stood on the side and ran the scrubber, tethered by a rope to a group up top to keep man and machine from slipping to the bottom. Another person tossed soap powder in front of the scrubber, while yet another ran the hose to rinse soap and dirt down to the bottom. At least three other people held the electric wire high so as not to contact the water and electrocute the entire crew. When clean, the filling with water took about a week because the well only had a 1" pipe. During this time, the kids who didn't swim well would enjoy the low water level. Mil and Fran also had a two room cabin near the pool with a pool table and room for dancing, ping pong, parties and so forth. [This was the cabin Betty Bollinger remembers having catechism classes once a week for the Catholic children in the neighborhood.] Their old horse, Patsy could pull a buggy and we had a nice one. Often Mildred drove Patsy to Sitman's Drug Store with several of us kids and her collie dog named 'Shag'. Our dog Sarge would run alongside as the buggy was full. Mil bought all the kids and dogs ice cream cones from the old fashioned soda fountain inside. Even in those days we turned some heads on Highland Road because horse and buggy travel was a rare sight. About every seven years or so we had snow in the deep south (we called it snow but it was really sleet that packs into ice balls, not snowballs). We would use corrugated sheet metal with one kid in front, bending up the leading edge on the hill on Dubois. We used the same sheet metal to convert the front wheels of the buggy into runners the year it sleeted while we had Patsy, improvising socks for Patsy from feed sacks.

"Every year on Christmas Eve Mil and Fran had a large fireworks display across the street from their house on Dubois. It was preceded by a large group of residents caroling throughout the neighborhood. For the kids, it was mandatory to carol in order to attend the fireworks display. I recall being extremely jealous of the older people who were chosen to light the fireworks until finally I qualified. Sometimes it was necessary to go back in the woods to put out a fire started by a wayward rocket ....fortunately, the snakes were dormant that time of year. How fortunate we were to have Mildred Dubois and Fran Burns.

"At Halloween, Mil and Fran would welcome trick or treat kids. They wouldn't just put treats in their bags and send them on their way but insisted that they come in and asked to do something for their treat – sing, dance, play the piano, tell a funny story, do a trick, etc. Parents were also invited in and all enjoyed punch and cookies. Of course there were the pranks that became traditions in the neighborhood. Who didn't raid pears from Windham's pear trees on Sunset Blvd. Every year many of us would soap Frank Carroll's garage windows on the corner of Leeward and Chandler while some of the group were collecting treats at the front door . . . the daddy of all annual pranks was chopping down a small tree and running it up the flagpole at

Highland School. We always had someone like Jimmy Sturgis shinny up the pole pushing the little chain as high as possible so Wilbur the janitor would need a ladder to lower the tree. [Bill Stracener recalls that his older brother, along with Bob Childress and Bob Kreager dismantled a buggy that belonged to the Haases on Highland Road, climbed onto their roof and re-assembled it there. Of course the pranksters were tracked down and made to restore the buggy to its rightful place.] With George and Jim Sturgis, my brother and I made up the SSG (Secret Swamp Gang). We loved the Acres with a passion and didn't want it to change so we would take down every 'For Sale' sign on vacant lots and hide them in the top of Sturgis's garage. For many years, the circle in front of the school was one big open area which many people thought would be a park. When houses were built there we were devastated. In the early years there were no houses on the east side of Chandler Drive from Leeward to Sunset. The grass grew like hay and periodically a tractor would cut the grass leaving lots of loose hay that we would construct teepees with the aid of poles and smoke corn silk in corncob pipes – what a fire hazard! Another hazard was the tree house, complete with trap door, lockable from the inside, using four cypress trees that we found didn't sway in the wind in unison and soon became unsafe and had to be abandoned.

"The early phones were on a party-line system and we always had enough very young kids who didn't understand that an incoming call for us had our distinctive ring, and would answer, holding up the caller. Phone numbers were only four digits on the rotary phone, then gradually as digits were added, we finally had the Dickens exchange prefix. Progress hasn't always been attractive with some things bringing mixed blessings. Those years in the Acres are most cherished and I wouldn't trade them for all my other places of residence including Arizona, Alaska and Hawaii". Jim DeGeneres will stir a lot of memories for the "old timers".

XI

Julia Hawkins looks back and recalls some outstanding contributors to the neighborliness of the Acres. Besides the "unofficial mayor" Bill Burbank there was Stanley Gross who was on the City Parish Council and worked for the improvement of the area, including street lighting in the Acres. He and his brother-in-law Leonard Gremillion had the State Lumber Co. on Highland Road and their wives, Fenie and Mary were a great asset to the community. Ned and Jerry Hickel at 657 Sunset Blvd. in the old Parker house have been in the Acres all their married life and with their great family have added so much. Ned, of Esso/Exxon, was a Boy Scout leader and a senior Olympian chosen as the 'Olympian of the year" one year. Myra and Jordan Lee moved into 457 Nelson Drive right after WWII and had four sons – their maid used to say that a woman who has four boys is as good as a man! Jordan taught bio-chemistry at LSU and his father was Dean of the School of Agriculture. Myra taught for many years at Highland School - a much loved and respected family. Leon and Margaret Calvit moved to 444 Nelson in 1958 and raised a wonderful family at a home that has the prettiest mimosa tree in the Acres!. One of their sons is now living on 216 Nelson, Mark and Jeannine. Mark is the manager of Southside Gardens Retirement home where many of our neighbors are now living – Mildred Evans, Jean and Jacques deTarnovsky, Heartease Higgins and Bill Swyers. On Julia's special list were 'Chuck' and Ruth Dillemuth who had adopted six children and still found time to help the neighborhood. June Lank talks of the "spirit of the Acres": "Hurricane Betsy in 1965 toppled trees and power was out all over town – yards were blocked with limbs and debris. Besides the mess, the weather was hot and sticky, the children were fussy, and we felt discouraged and helpless. Sometime that morning, we heard a power saw – a pretty rare tool in those days – working on our street. We perked up thinking that the city was really out and on top of things. As the noise came closer, we were amazed to see Chuck Dillemuth and his son working their way down the street, clearing yards and making roads passable – doing something to help the neighbors. We will never forget what hope and cheer he brought us with his simple act. That, to us, was what "Life in the Acres" was all about". Chuck Dillemuth ran for Senate on the Nixon ticket against Jimmy Morrison, and was later chosen as a Golden Deeds Recipient and everyone who knew him understood why, says Julia. Their son Bob, with Paula, live at 5848 Guava Drive in the family home. Red and Tina Wratten, Irvin and Silvia (she an artist and he a Dean at LSU), were among the many who come to mind as wonderful neighbors, and also Hazel and J. Burton LeBlanc at 825 Dubois. Loretta Spaht who also lived at 888 Dubois reminisced about her thirty years in the Acres and "loved every minute of her life there and wished she could live it all over again." There are many family relations represented, like the Creeds, the Prescotts, the Patricks but the prize for the most "togetherness" family goes to the Bourgoynes – Ted, who was Dean of the School of Engineering, and Kathy on Boone raised their children here. Now daughters Tammy and Tracy live on Chandler and Leeward, and Darryl and Brad with their families live on Leeward also. That's family togetherness! Another remarkable family Julia recalls, was the Harrison Bagwells at 5811 Menlo. Altogether, three Acres residents have run for the Governorship of Louisiana, Harrison Bagwell, Fred Dent, and Carlos Spaht who was remembered by Myra Lee as being so courteous and gentlemanly riding his horse around the neighborhood asking for their support in his campaign. "Harrison ran for Governor on the Republican ticket back in the days when there weren't too many of them around! He didn't win, of course, in the Democrat Louisiana of the Long era but his Acres neighbors felt he would have made a great governor."

The Bagwells started the Halloween SUPPER! They served hot dogs and root beer at their house as a treat (with later repercussions). When a terrible fire destroyed their home, they lived in a rented trailer on the grounds to supervise the rebuilding, and neighbors gave a shower to help replenish their home. We remember our children making maps and planning their trick-or-treat routes so they could get to every house in time" recalls Julia. Betty Bollinger used to go to Mrs. Bateman's "to see if she was still giving kumquats for treats, and she always was – Nanette Kirby had apple bobbing in her front yard and Judge Carlos Spaht gave nickel candy bars for treats!" Mildred Dubois would have a big bonfire in her yard and the children would have to do a 'turn' and of course their costumes would have to be judged (by Drs. Irving Berg and Giles Gray) to win the prizes for 'Best'. Nowadays the Civic Association holds a Halloween party for the children at the park on Leeward.

Bernadette Day takes over the story from Julia Hawkins: "We remember the beautiful April day in 1976 when we were looking for a house to buy and were shown what became our home at 5811 Menlo Drive. When we first saw it, we fell in love with the neighborhood and especially the huge 100-year-old-plus oak tree that graced the front yard. There was an albino squirrel looking at us quizzically that seemed to

Charles H. **Dillemuth** FOR CONGRESS
On the Nixon Ticket

MILDRED DuBOIS
for
City Council
Ward One

I Stand for
PROGRESS WITHOUT WASTE!

'ACRES CAMPAIGNERS'

SPAHT for Governor

HARRISON G. BAGWELL
Republican Candidate for Governor

If You THINK Republican
... VOTE Republican !

VOTE FOR HARRISON G. BAGWELL

for GOVERNOR

IN THE GENERAL ELECTION

Definitely Dent
Governor

Three neighbors who ran for
Governor of Louisiana

wink at us – we knew then that we were hooked. That albino squirrel was well known in the neighborhood and became a great pet. Shortly after we moved in, we were puzzled on our first Halloween when every kid who was trick or treating asked, "Where are the hot dogs"? When we said we only had candy to give away, the kids invariably departed in disappointment. Only later did we learn that we had broken a sacred Acres tradition! The previous owners, the Bagwells, had faithfully served hot dogs to the neighborhood at Halloween. We also learned that we created a great demand for the annual hotdog Halloween party at Menlo Park because "the Days were no longer serving hot dogs." We had company shortly after we moved in and were rocking on the front porch, discussing the rabbits, squirrels, ducks and birds we'd been seeing. Suddenly a small horse raced through the yard, speeding straight for us followed by five cute little kids. That memorable afternoon we were stunned and scared by the extraordinary appearance of a tiny horse that was fast enough to win the Triple Crown and quickly ran into the house. We and our guests have never forgotten how impressed we were with "all the wildlife" so apparent in the Acres. One regrettable memory was the calm, beautiful Mardi Gras day in the early 90's when that massive old oak tree – which had stood since William McKinley was in the White House – simply rolled over and died. Winston was in the back yard raking leaves when he heard a massive crash. Racing to the front, he encountered several neighbors also searching for the source of something that shook the earth. There was the old tree pitifully lying on its side and exposing its rotted center. A symbol of the Acres died that day, and for weeks thereafter we often found neighbors parked in front or in the driveway quietly mourning its loss."

XII

The Acres residents have suffered a polio epidemic, fires, floods, snows and the big freeze of 1961, hurricanes and drought that have taken their toll, and on the pecans, magnolias, oaks and other trees and beautiful shrubs. Through it all, we are reminded of the ebb and flow of life. There has been tragedy and there has been joy; and as Annabelle Armstrong remarked, there are few, if any, subdivisions with a school, that have the rich history that has been recorded from its early beginnings. The more recent residents are, in these days, making a life of Acres Memories for themselves, not as yet set down for posterity. What is so obvious in this collection of memories is that the families and generations who have called University Acres home, retain a great affection for this beautiful spot and the beautiful friendships that it has harbored. Its residents retain a love for its timelessness and the part that it has played in their lives.

* * * * * * *

Julia Hawkins, the Acres historian, researched and made contact with residents past and present and collected information and anecdotes for this memoir. Constance Navratil compiled and wrote the text, and both wish to extend their gratitude to the many friends who contributed their precious Acres memories for the happy recollection of us all. A special note of gratitude is made to Robert Rackley for his generous printing of this publication.

Photographs were contributed by Barry Bagwell, Polly Blanche, Randy Burbank, Tommy Campbell, Jamie Carruth, Blanche Cretini, Jim and Don DeGeneres, Fred Dent, Janelle Earle, Don Fuson, Nelson Goings, Pat Gremillion, Stephany Gross, Frances Harvey, Julia Hawkins, Bunny Hines, Ruth Hyatt, Kelly Johnson, John Kent, Alice Bankston Michael, Ruth Murray, Nancy Murrill, Constance Navratil, Prewitt Nelson, Joe Richard, Loretta Spaht, Bill Stracener, Cookie Odom West and Highland School Scrapbook.

Julia Hawkins   Constance Navratil

* * * * * * * * * * * *

Baton Rouge, 2004

Bas-reliefs inspired
By Aesop's Fables
Adorn the Main Entrance
Of Highland School

ADDENDUM

Principals at Highland Elementary

Myrtie Polizotto	Thonsa Rice	Betty Matens
Geraldine Wall	Don Ray Beard	Nannie Kinchen

Partial List of Teachers at Highland Elementary

*Ruby Babin	*Helen Grenier	*Sarah Powell - Secry.
*Geneva Bateman	Lil Harper	*Maxine Richardson
Juanita Bishop	*Barbara Haygood	*Eleanor Roberts
Diane Bumgartner	Edith Hilton	Camilla Rachal
Jimmy Cash	*Pat Hines - Secry.	Jerry Scallan
Linda Chambers	*Joy Johnson	Elaine Scriber
Mac Chauvan	Mary Helen Jones	Fran Schrnbckle
*Ora Childress	Gabe Jumonville	Betsy Shea
Marjory Dean	Eloise Landry	Elaine Simon
Cynthia Donahue	Lu Lastrapes	*Violet Stracener
Edith Draper	*Myra Lee	Tot Swanson
Nan Dry	Jake Leitsner	Mona Terry
Ellen Ervin	Mary Lou Loudon	Dot Turner
Mildred Eubanks	C. G. McGee	*Ava Ulmer
Roseland Fagan	Catherine Martin	*Edna West
Karen Farr	*Earline Nolan	*Emily Willett
*Garnet Glasgow	Olivet O'Conner	*Louise Willett
*Jeanne Grenchik	Sarah Parsons	Virginia Worley

*Lived in The Acres

University Acres Residents Who Were Reading Friends at Highland Elementary 2001-2004

Nel Bailey	Nelson Goings	Tomi Morton
Jennifer Bollinger	Ann Guissinger	Ruth Murray
Jeannine Calvit	John Henderson	Nancy Murrill
Margaret Calvit	Nathalie Henderson	Constance Navratil
Carolyn Cavanaugh	Ann Legett	Julie Sears
Michael Cavanaugh	Marcia Marsh	Beverly Langlois
Brigitte Delzell	Boots McArdle	Mag Wall
Lloyd Frye	Frank McArdle	
Elizabeth Goings	Becky Melancon	

Generations in The Acres!

Children of University Acres Folks Who Lived or Are Living in the Acres

Dan, son of Bill Bankhead
Beverly, Daughter of Bryant Bateman
Billy, son of Malcolm Bollinger
Brad, son of Ted Bourgoyne
Darryl, son of Ted Bourgoyne
Tammy, daughter of Ted Bourgoyne
Tracey, daughter of Ted Bourgoyne
Bill, son of William Burbank
Mark, son of Leon Calvit
Tommy, son of Joe Campbell
Jane, daughter of Red Evans
Lloyd, son of J. B. Frye
Hugh, son of Leslie Glasgow
Ann, daughter of Stanley Gross
Stephanie, daughter of Stanley Gross
Bill, son of Robert Hines
Warren, son of Oscar Kimbler

Bill, son of John Matthews
Rebecca, daughter of Bill Matthews
Frankie, son of Frank McArdle
Doug, son of Al Moreau
Whit, son of Paul Murrill
Billy, son of Bill Patrick
Ben, son of Tomas Payne
Lauren, daughter of James Pierson
Bill, son of W. A. Prescott
Bobby, son of W. A. Prescott
John, son of Bob Scearce
Sharon, daughter of Nona Walker
Sissy, daughter of William Wall
Kathi, daughter of Walter Whitehead
Pam, daughter of Martin Wooden
Nicholas, son of A. N. Yiannopoulous

Grandchildren of University Acres Folks Who Lived or Are Living in The Acres

Mary Lollie Aulet, granddaughter of J. B. Frye
Laure Burgess, granddaughter of Pat Hine
Shawn Kirby, grandson of Gerorge Kirby
Mary Kate Valuzzo, granddaughter of Sadie Oliver
Davin Spring, grandson of Sadie Oliver
Janelle Earle, granddaughter of Mary Jane Rupp
Rebecca Matthews, granddaughter of Nona Walker

University Acres Folks Who Have Moved to St. James Place

Melva Bannerman
Silvia & Irvin Berg
Irene Burbank
Helen & Harry Bushnell
Helen & Joe Campbell

Olita Hathaway
Pat Hines
Joy Johnson
June & Bob Lank
Helen & Jerry Law

Mr. and Mrs. C. L. Lerner
Lille Mae Moreau
Sadie Oliver
Jackie Richard
Eleanor Roberts

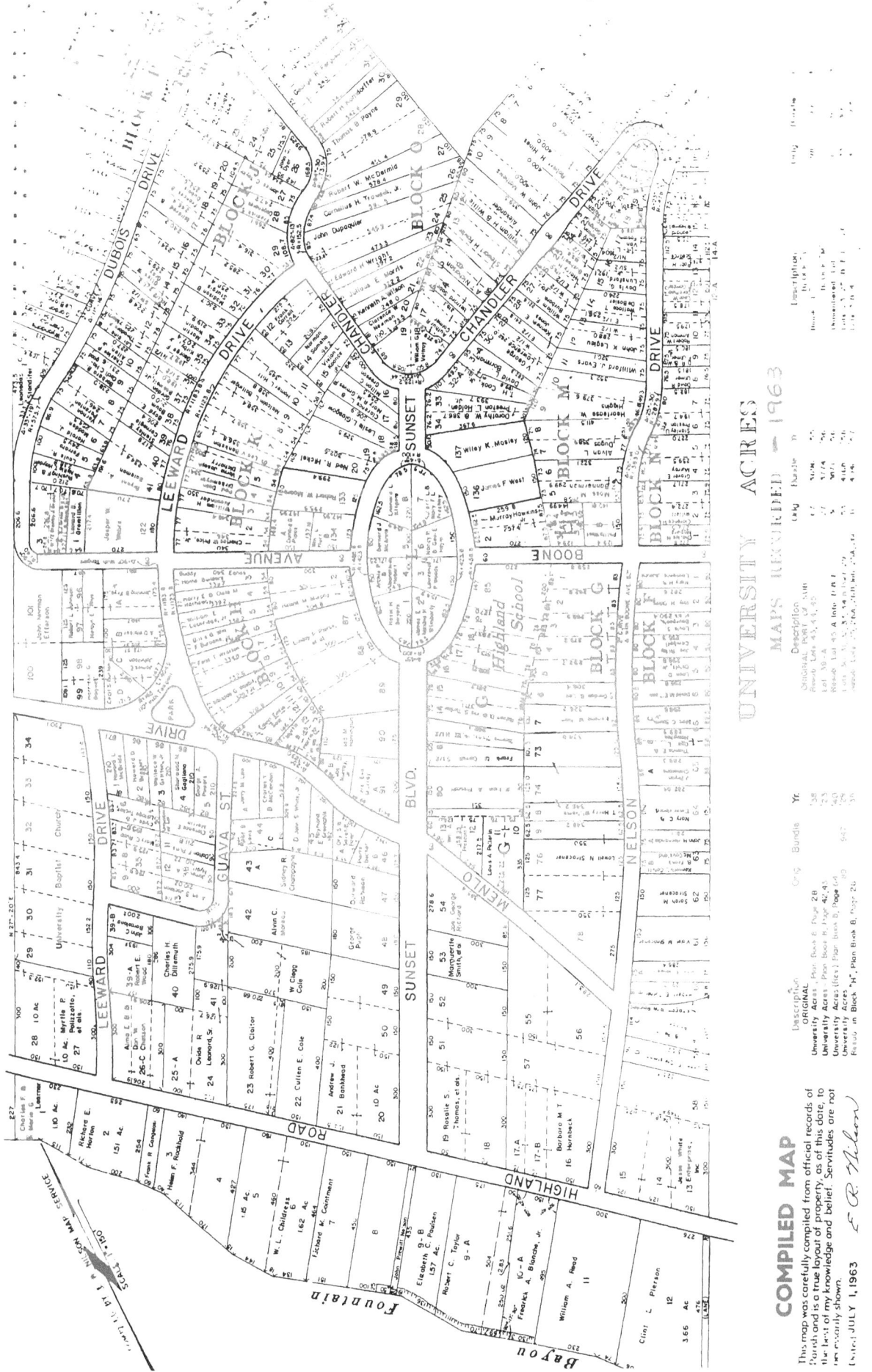

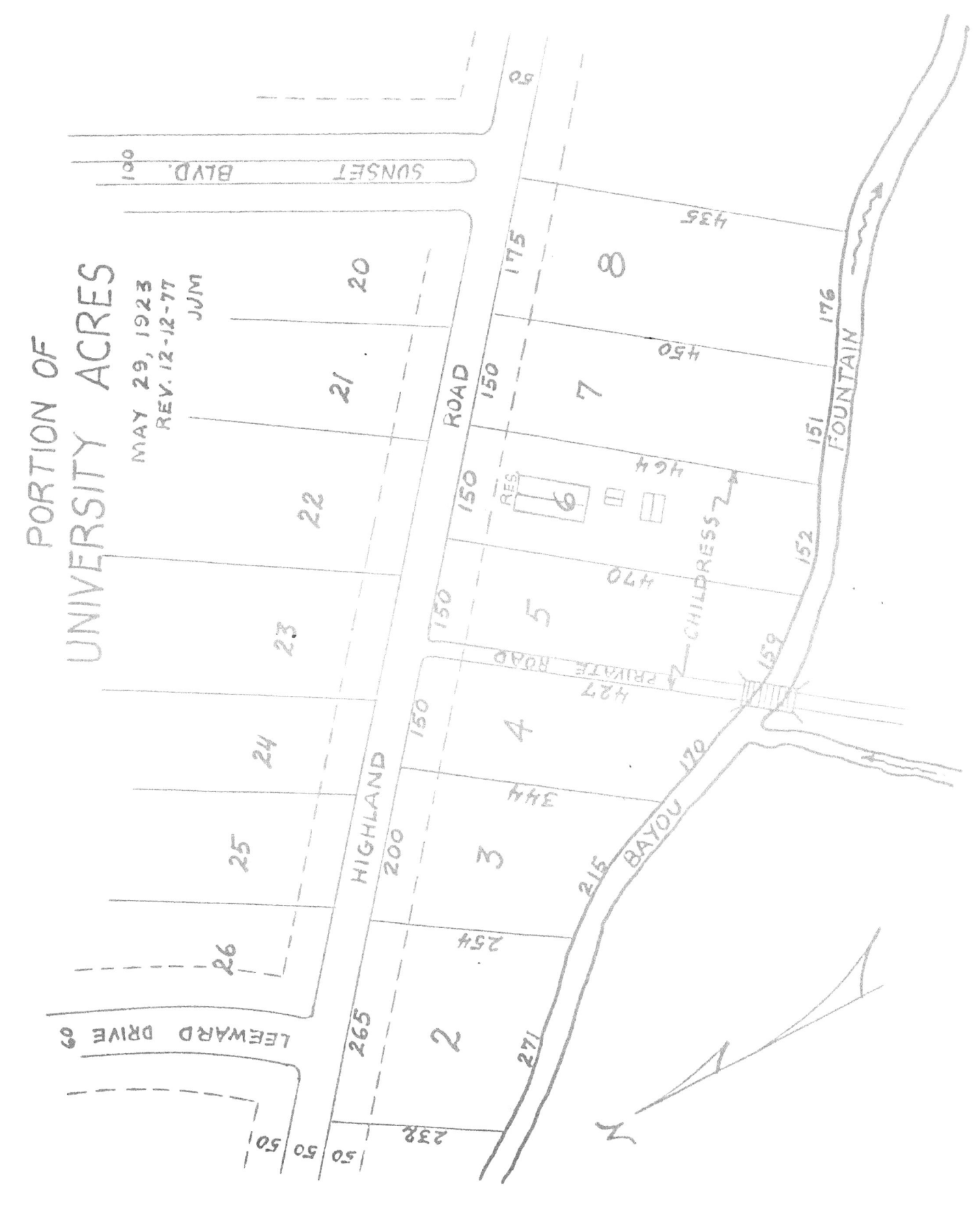

MAP OF
UNIVERSITY ACRES
LAID OUT FOR
PELICAN REALTY CO.